THE FREEDOM MODEL FOR THE FAMILY

BY MICHELLE DUNBAR

WITH STEVEN SLATE & MARK SCHEEREN

TABLE OF CONTENTS

THE FREEDOM MODEL FOR THE FAMILY

This book provides an overview of *The Freedom Model for Addictions*. It is directed specifically to those who love someone who is struggling with substance use problems (i.e., addiction). It is a great tool for family members, friends, and loved ones who want to learn quickly about the Freedom Model approach and how vastly different it is from drug and alcohol treatment programs. This book provides a completely unique, common sense approach to addiction and helping your loved one, while also focusing on how you can improve your own life. If your loved one is reading *The Freedom Model for Addictions*, is enrolled in The Freedom Model Private Instruction, or is attending one of our Retreats, and you are seeking a more in-depth analysis, we recommend that you read *The Freedom*

Model for Addictions, which is available for order in print and digital editions with all major online retailers, including Amazon, Barnes & Noble, Google Play, etc. If you are reading this book because you are seeking help for a loved one and are not sure in which direction to turn, this book can provide you with factual, data-driven information so you can make a fully informed decision. If, after reading through The Freedom Model for the Family, you have questions or would like to inquire about what help may be available for you or your loved one, you can call to talk with one of our caring consultants at 1-888-424-2626.

INTRODUCTION:

THERE IS A SOLUTION

Being close to someone who is struggling with substance use problems can be exhausting and overwhelming at times. The problem commonly referred to as "addiction" is grossly misunderstood and the misinformation being propagated by addiction experts and the treatment and recovery community is misleading, wrong, and harmful. By labeling problem substance use (i.e. addiction) a progressive, incurable disease, this idea systematically takes away the substance user's ability to change. Worse yet, by labeling it a "family disease", the responsibility for the substance user's behaviors are basically taken away from the only person who does have control, the substance user, and placed on those who have no power at all over the substance user's behaviors, the family. This family addiction disease theory, and the treatment based on it, is largely inaccurate and leads to damaged relationships and broken families.

3

If you have attended any kind of therapy, especially family addiction therapy, you are likely familiar with the terms "denial", "co-dependent", and "enabling." You have probably analyzed each of your actions and reactions to see how you may be contributing to the substance user's ongoing drug and/or alcohol problems. You may feel immense guilt over your past behaviors and conflicts with the substance user as you are concerned those may have contributed to the substance user's behaviors today. You may be struggling with intense fear and anxiety for the substance user's health and well-being, both mentally and physically, and you may now be completely confused as to what you should do. (*All of these common personal struggles experienced by the family are addressed fully later in this text.*)

In these situations, well-meaning family members, friends, counselors, and even acquaintances, weigh in on what they think you should do and each person's advice is different and many times conflicting. This can leave you more confused and frustrated than ever. So, what should you do? The answer may be simpler than you think and this book will help you to determine the best course of action for you and your family. For each family, the answer is different. And even for individuals within the same family, the best course of action may be different from one person to the next. First and foremost, it is important to strip away the misinformation and ensure that everyone involved learns the truth about addiction, substance use, and choice.

As you will read in this book, the misinformation being propagated in our addiction disease and recovery-centered culture is at the heart of the current addiction crisis and is actually fueling it. The addiction disease theory, and the treatment based on it, makes people believe that they need to be rescued. It forces them to think they must be saved from themselves by external means. Heavy substance users are taught that something outside of themselves, a sponsor, a counselor, a pill, a meeting, a treatment provider, etc., must get into their mind and change their wants and desires largely against their wishes. And they are taught that their wants and desires for heavy substance use are not only morally wrong, but an indicator that they are sick and completely out of control, which is why they need an outside entity to fix them.

One of the primary problems with addiction treatment is the reality that the only person that can change your wants and desires is you. Think about something you truly love - maybe it's coffee, chocolate, Chardonnay, or running. Can some external force change your desire for that which you love? In the same vein, can an external force make you like or love something that you don't? No, it can't; that kind of preference change can only happen within your own mind. And that internal change of mind is absolutely required for people to change their substance use habits for good.

Research has shown clearly that no one makes a long term change in behavior, and in their preferences, based on lies, distortions, and fear; and sadly, the treatment industry is built on those things. It is built on forcing people to make a change they don't truly want to make. The truth is people will only make a change in their lives when they come to believe they can be happier by making the change. You may think, well, isn't that the same thing as wanting to avoid negative consequences? As you read through this book, I hope you will see the immense differences between these two motivators, moving toward happiness and avoiding pain, and exactly why that difference is crucial to your loved one's long term success.

The overall goal of the The Freedom Model for the Family is to educate the family on what addiction is, what it is not ,and how people stop and/or change their substance use habits. We also want to help families separate their own happiness, success, and life goals from the substance user's. Ultimately,The Freedom Model for the Family is designed to help families of substance users build happier lives, regardless of what the substance user does or does not do. While it is true that you have no control over the substance user and his/her behavior, it is important to understand that, by changing the relationship you currently have with the substance user and improving the quality of your own life, it is more likely the substance user will come to you for help when ready, potentially follow your example, and seek to improve the quality of his/her life as well.

CHAPTER 1:

WHAT IS THE FREEDOM MODEL?

(This section is taken directly from Chapter 1 of The Freedom Model for Addictions and has been edited and adapted for this family book.)

The *Freedom Model for Addictions* is not a program, nor a process of recovery. It is not treatment, counseling, or therapy. Instead, it is a way of thinking about the choices people can and will make in their own lives. It is an approach about a confused idea called addiction and recovery, and it seeks to clear the air on these constructs. The Freedom Model debunks all the addiction and recovery myths so people can freely and happily choose how they wish to proceed with respect to their substance use. The goal is for people to make that decision based on factual information and what they believe will bring them greater happiness, rather than a hollow decision based on lies, distortions, and fear.

The current cultural views of addiction as a disease, that substances have supernatural powers to enslave people, and the treatment that corresponds to these views seek to force people into abstinence from all substances. Treatment providers do this in various ways, but primarily through fear based motivators, most of which are completely false and illogical.

When substance users arrive for help in the addiction and recovery world, they are immediately told they must never touch a single dose of alcohol or other drugs for the rest of their lives. They are told if they do, then they will consume substances uncontrollably until they end up in jail, another rehab, or dead. While data overwhelmingly disproves this assertion, the purpose of telling it to substance users is to make their decision to abstain a "no-brainer". The results of these fraudulent fear mongering tactics are evident all around you. The rates of people dying from overdose are increasing exponentially at a time when treatment is more readily available than at any point in our history. And the data shows that substance users are at their greatest risk of overdose within the first few weeks and months after leaving rehab or treatment, where the powerlessness idea was forced upon them.

By only giving substance users a binary set of options, abstinence or heavy use, and using the lie of loss of control to scare people into abstinence, the real issue of why the individual is using is never addressed. The fact is people continue to use because they have a preference for being high or drunk. They developed this preference for their own, personal reasons. All substance users, regardless of their level of use, continue to use because they believe they are getting benefits from using substances. And they believe they can be happier using at that particular level than by reducing it or abstaining from use altogether.

Instead of tackling their preference head-on, within the current treatment model, fear and panic rule their decision making process. Think of it this way, if a mugger catches you in an alleyway, pulls out a gun, and gives you the ultimatum "your money or your life," is it really a positive decision when you hand over your wallet? Of course not. It's a coerced decision, one that you make begrudgingly, and one that you regret and resent having to make. The ultimatum, "abstinence or your life", is much the same. It is a coerced decision made out of fear, panic, and other negative emotions. It is one where the pursuit of happiness is made irrelevant.

The scientific evidence is clear, nobody "loses control" of their substance use, not even the most extreme users. (For a complete breakdown of this point, see Appendix A in *The Freedom Model for Addictions*.) If people don't actually lose control, then this means that they are capable of using moderately. This is a simple logical conclusion based on facts and born out of research (e.g., 50% of former "alcoholics" become moderate drinkers). (For supporting documentation, see Appendix E in *The Freedom Model for Addictions*). Yet treatment providers insist on telling substance users that they have a disease or allergy that causes them to lose control over their drug and alcohol use. They do this because it's a convenient shortcut by which they can coerce the individual into immediately agreeing to the abstinence goal that has been chosen for them.

The difference between the addiction counselor and the mugger is this: the mugger is forcing a one-time decision, but the counselors are trying to force a lifelong decision. It's no wonder this tactic has such high failure rates. People end up miserable while abstaining, feeling deprived of joy, feeling coerced into behaving in a way they don't want to behave, until they eventually go back to the old pattern of heavy substance use, and, in many cases, they begin using at heavier rates than prior to treatment. After all, in addition to being taught that they will lose control, they are also taught their disease is progressive and, because of this, their usage will increase, regardless of their length of time abstinent, and their problems will escalate exponentially as well.

In The Freedom Model, your loved one will be presented with all of their options: 1. continued heavy use, 2. adjusted substance use (moderate use), and 3. abstinence. We understand that informing your loved one of these options may instantly strike fear and dread in your heart as the hope of most people close to heavy substance users is that the substance user will become and stay abstinent forever. The abstinence goal makes perfect sense to you, as you have likely watched your loved one struggle with substance use for years. He may have lost jobs, a marriage, custody of children. He may have developed health issues and had one or more trips to the hospital for an overdose, a fall, accident, or illness related to substance use.

You may be thinking, but my father is a "real alcoholic", who drinks continuously and has pancreatitis and liver damage. You may be concerned that your daughter has already overdosed twice and you are terrified she won't be so lucky the next time. You may be thinking that your son has been arrested for stealing to support his habit, is facing prison time if he messes up again, and you're wondering how it can possibly be helpful to tell people with severe substance use problems that they can moderate. The answer is quite simple: we must tell them because it's the truth. By avoiding the truth, we would be intentionally trying to bypass the critical step of them honestly evaluating their preference for heavy substance use and examining the real potential for greater happiness in those other two options, moderation and abstinence.

Remember, in treatment programs and the recovery society, substance users are told there are only two options: complete abstinence or uncontrollable usage that leads to institutions, jails, and death. This is a complete lie, and sadly, becomes a self-fulfilling prophecy for far too many people, as seen in the increased rates of binge usage, heavy usage, and overdoses post-treatment. In treatment, substance users are told this, while also being told that relapse is part of recovery. This is a very important point: in treatment, and our current recovery culture (including 12 Step meetings like AA & NA), substance users are told that they have a progressive, incurable brain disease that renders them forever powerless over substances. At the same time, they are also told they must choose to be completely abstinent from all substances. This requires them to make a daily choice to not use substances, while at the same time, having to admit and accept that they are powerless over substances, and then they are told that relapse (using substances) is part of lifelong recovery and is to be expected. So they are powerless, but must make a daily choice to abstain? Because this illogical nonsense is so ingrained in our culture, you may need to read through it a few times to fully recognize the inherent problems within it. This erroneous treatment protocol is clearly a recipe for the crisis we are seeing today.

The actual data, as collected through large government studies over the past several years, is consistent. It shows that more than 90% of "alcoholics" get over the problem, with more than half moderating their alcohol use to non-problematic levels. More than 97% of people who struggle with heavy marijuana use get over the problem, and more than 99% of cocaine users get over the problem. The vast majority of people who get over these problems do not go to treatment, and more than half are not completely abstinent from all substances. (*For detailed information and supporting documentation about this data, please read Chapter 1, The Freedom Model for Addictions. There is also data for heroin and other opiates in The Freedom Model, Appendix D, "Heroin and the Myth of Addictiveness".*) By providing substance users factual information, we're opening the door to them being able to make a fully informed decision. What treatment does not tell people, and what many people fail to understand, is that substance users can be happy in abstinence. They can be happy in some reduction in usage or a switch to safer substances. In the Freedom Model, this is the primary focus - to have our readers and guests explore the possibility that they can find happiness in these options. Our readers and retreat guests learn exactly how people change their substance use habits and maintain that change indefinitely.

If you think back on your own life, I'm certain you can think of people you knew, or perhaps it was you, who were heavy substance users but then simply made a change. Those self-changers didn't go to meetings, counseling, or treatment; they just stopped their heavy, problematic substance use. Those people are among the vast majority. They change because they change their priorities, preferences, and desires. They come to believe that they can be happier by reducing their substance use or stopping it altogether. And this is exactly how all people stop their addictions, whether they go to treatment or not. They come to believe they can be happier with less of the substance or with none at all. Sadly, in treatment, this fundamental requirement for making a change is not addressed at all and thus any changes that people make are, more often than not, very short-lived.

Those who come to see a change as genuinely happier and more satisfying than their previous problematic style of substance use change rapidly and maintain the change happily. This is most directly achieved by re-assessing the relative benefits of various levels of substance use, including abstinence. Happiness is front and center in the decision-making process.

DOES THE FREEDOM MODEL TELL MY LOVED ONE TO MODERATE?

One of the greatest misunderstandings of The Freedom Model approach is that, because we say moderate substance use is possible for anyone, that means we are saying that people should moderate. This is not the case at all. *The Freedom Model for Addictions* does not advocate any level of substance use, but instead seeks to provide factual information. Throughout The Freedom Model text, we talk about the inherent risks in substance use at all levels and we also directly challenge the benefits people perceive they are getting from substances. The purpose of telling people that there is no loss of control, and that moderate use is possible, is to allow the substance user to make a fully informed decision based on facts and moving toward greater happiness, and not on lies, distortions, and fear.

The Freedom Model for Addictions, and everyone at Baldwin Research Institute, Inc., and the Freedom Model Retreats, remain completely neutral on whether or not anyone should use substances at any level. It is not our intent to tell people what personal decisions they should make, or to deny or grant permission to anyone to use substances. Counselors who tell people what they should do, end up depriving the substance user of the chance to take ownership of their decisions and figure out what they really want to do. As educators, our job is simply to present the truth about substance use so that people can make their own informed decision about it. Here are two very important truths:

> **1.** Moderate use is possible for anyone, because loss of control is a myth.
>
> **2.** Risk-free substance use is not possible for anyone.

Every action in life carries some level of risk and cost. It is up to each person to be aware and decide what level of risks and costs are acceptable to them.

BELIEFS ARE POWERFUL

We make this point absolutely clear to substance users throughout the text: if you are a believer in addiction and recovery, you should never attempt to moderate or use at all. That statement makes sense, considering adherence to the belief in powerlessness directly correlates with heavy, problematic substance use. We make it clear that if the substance user believes that there are a class of people called "addicts" that cannot stop ingesting a substance once they start, then they should abstain. We tell substance users that if they have any doubts regarding the existence of free will and if they believe that, on some level, substances have the power to enslave users, then their attempts to moderate will be undermined by their skepticism and faulty belief system.

Free will is an absolute. Either people have it or they don't. They behave exactly as they believe they will. The goal of The Freedom Model is to challenge those beliefs that substances are powerful and that substance users cross a line where they become powerless addicts. The goal of this family book is to debunk those myths for you as well, so you can make informed decisions for your own life and for your relationship with your loved one moving forward.

WILL THE FREEDOM MODEL FOR ADDICTIONS WORK FOR MY LOVED ONE?

This is the number one question asked of our consultants and staff when taking calls from family members just like you, so it is appropriate to address it immediately. While this question may mean different things to different people, for most callers, the question means, "Will The Freedom Model make and keep my loved one sober and drug free forever?" We understand that is typically the goal for family members and friends when they send their loved one into a treatment or rehab program. The simple answer to that question is no, there is no program, no treatment, no medication, no meeting, nor is there a person with the power to make your loved one choose not to drink or use drugs, not while they are in a program or treatment, and certainly not once they've completed it.

If you are close to someone you believe has a substance use problem, you've likely spent many hours trying to persuade that person to reduce or stop their substance use entirely. You've probably told this person that you are worried about their health and safety. You've told them how their behavior when drunk or high has negatively affected you, and you've probably had more than one argument or altercation with this individual about their substance use. They know you don't like it. They know their substance use upsets you, someone they care about deeply, and they know that it's dangerous, yet none of this has resulted in that person making a change.

Perhaps your loved one has already been to one or more treatment programs, multiple 12 Step group meetings, counseling sessions, or therapists, and he is still using substances heavily. For many substance users, their substance use escalates after they go to treatment. Additionally, their binge usage becomes more frequent and their behavior in other areas may become more erratic. This is all due to the primary goal of treatment, counseling, and 12 Step meetings which is to convince substance users they are sick and powerless, and thus must abstain from all substance use based on lies and fear, rather than through having them honestly assess what they want.

In addition, in recent years, more and more heavy substance users are diagnosed with mental health disorders as well. The most commonly diagnosed disorders being major depressive disorder (depression), generalized anxiety disorder, bi-polar disorder, borderline personality disorder, and attention deficit disorder (ADD). With these diagnoses often comes psychoactive medications that affect brain chemistry and add a new wrinkle into the equation. For many substance users, their mental health symptoms are the result of heavy substance use, and therefore can be remedied by adjusting or stopping their usage and taking care of their personal responsibilities. By giving the substance user a mental health diagnosis, and then telling them that their mental health disorder is causing their substance use, this can further escalate substance use problems. Being told that your mental health issue is causing your heavy substance use, but then also being told that you must stop substance use to fix your mental health issue, is a circular problem that provides no viable way out of either. The truth is, according to the latest statistics, only one 1 in 5 people with a mental illness also have a substance use problem, which means 4 out of 5 do not respond to their mental illness by using substances heavily. (Center for Behavioral Health Statistics and Quality, 2016). (Supposed causes of addiction are addressed later in this book and fully in *The Freedom Model for Addictions*.)

Sadly, those who take on the belief that they are powerless and diseased have reduced rates of changing their substance use patterns. (For research and supporting documentation, see *The Freedom Model for Addictions*, Chapter 1.) This indoctrination into the powerlessness belief is the primary reason why treatment doesn't work. It does not allow for people to get over the problem permanently and it doesn't address the reasons why the person uses substances. The goal of treatment is much like the movie "Reefer Madness" from the 1930's; it is to scare people into not using substances by giving substances supernatural powers to enslave people. You may have heard the slogan, "keep it green", in rehab and recovery circles. The purpose of this slogan is to remind substance users to remember how awful their lives were when using -- remember it was all bad, wink, wink, nudge, nudge.

The problem is it wasn't all bad. If it was, nobody would use for very long, if at all. And, more importantly, if fear of negative consequences worked to make people stop using, then the first time someone got violently ill after a night of heavy drinking, got arrested for possession, or experienced withdrawal symptoms from heroin, they wouldn't use again, but they do. They do because, to them, there is some good. They do because they believe they are getting some benefits from using and that is the key.

That is why The Freedom Model, first and foremost, seeks to debunk the damaging myths that heavy substance users have a disease and are, therefore, powerless to stop or adjust their substance use. This false theory is a distraction. Once the disease theory is fully debunked, the text gets to the heart of the matter: what does this person like about using substances? What are the benefits they perceive they are getting from it? You see, it is only when the substance user begins to think critically about what it is she likes about her substance use, that she can even begin to ascertain whether she can and will be happier without it.

So, to answer your question, will *The Freedom Model for Addictions* work for my loved one, please know that it will provide your loved one with factual information so he/she can make an informed decision moving forward while shedding the myths that have kept them stuck. It will show your loved one that he is capable of making a lasting lifestyle change and can do so at any point in time. It will provide him with the truth about addiction, substance use, and recovery; that he is not diseased, and can make a change and leave those difficulties behind him forever. And it will show him exactly why he may feel like he's powerless and out of control, and why that is an illusion and not reality.

Finally, The Freedom Model will help your loved one to identify why she uses substances, so she can address the reason(s) directly, and make a decision on how she wants to proceed in her life based on what will make her happier. People make lasting changes in life based on moving toward happiness, not running from fear. It is for those reasons that The Freedom Model has significantly higher rates of long term success than treatment, and why your loved one will move forward in life armed with the information she needs to make a lasting lifestyle change.

It is our hope at Baldwin Research Institute that there will be a paradigm shift in this country away from the erroneous disease model of addiction, fear mongering, ineffective treatment methods, and the unholy marriage of treating heavy substance use as a disease and a crime simultaneously, toward non-judgmental, truth-based, educational methods that are far more compassionate and effective. Only then will we see rates of heavy substance use, dangerous binge usage, and tragic overdose deaths decrease.

CHAPTER 2:

WHAT IS ADDICTION?

Many people who are trying to help someone they love who is struggling with substance use become concerned and confused when they read through The Freedom Model website. They think, if addiction isn't a disease, does this mean that my loved one is choosing to be homeless, to crash his car, to lose his job and his family? Does it mean that my spouse loves alcohol more than me and our kids? Does it mean that my son's best friend wanted to die from a heroin overdose, or that my daughter wanted to get raped at that college party? These questions are understandable but they conflate two things: the desire to ingest substances and the outcomes that may or may not be a direct result of that substance use. Let me use an example to which most people can relate: you drive to work every day and you've gotten pretty comfortable on this drive. You do it without even thinking but, on one particular morning, you hit a patch of ice, lose control of your car, and hit a tree. Certainly you did not start out on that drive thinking, 'I'd like to hit a tree today'. No, you were only thinking that you would like to get to work that morning, yet your drive did not go as intended.

This is exactly the same for the substance user. Your brother may wish to go out for a night of drinking and partying with various substances. Just like the person that drives to work every day, your brother may make a habit of this behavior, and most nights work out just fine for him. Then, on one particular night, he gets some laced cocaine and has an adverse reaction. Thankfully, his friends call an ambulance and he is brought to the hospital. He didn't intend to end up in the hospital; that wasn't his goal when he was preparing to go out that night, when he was doing shots at the bar, or when he started doing lines in the bathroom. For the driver that hit that patch of ice, the risk of getting into an accident when driving is always there. The same is true for the substance user. There are always risks associated with ingesting substances. All substance users understand those risks and are willing to take them on when they make the choice to use, but that is far different than intending to have negative outcomes.

THE POSITIVE DRIVE PRINCIPLE

People choose to ingest substances for very specific personal reasons. They are not thinking, 'I would like to lose my family, my job, my freedom, or my life'. Those are usually not the goals or intent when they choose to use. Even if the individual has experienced negative consequences in the past, he/she is not thinking, 'I want bad things to happen to me'. They are thinking, 'I'd really like to have a drink, hit, or dose right now'. They are thinking that ingesting the substance will make them happier at that moment. The choice to use substances is always made in the pursuit of happiness.

This is an important point for you to consider and understand: people don't do things they genuinely don't want to do. They don't engage in behaviors or activities they believe have no value to them. And they certainly don't involuntarily go through all the steps it takes to plan out, procure, and ingest a substance. All people move in the direction they believe will make them happier. The Freedom Model calls this truth the Positive Drive Principle, or PDP, for short.

When we first discuss the PDP with our guests and their families, they usually question it. They provide examples of behaviors and activities that they find unpleasant or distasteful that they do in spite of hating: going to a job they don't like, changing their baby's diaper, or going to the dentist for a root canal. They think they have stumped us, but when you look at each of these activities, the person choosing to do them does see value in the activity. They believe going to that job they hate will make them happy because it provides money to pay for their home, food, and other things they find valuable. A mother or father changes their baby's diaper because they know it will make the baby comfortable, keep him from getting a painful rash and infection, and ultimately, a happy baby makes for a happy mommy and daddy. A person chooses to go get a root canal because they believe it will provide them some pain relief while keeping their tooth intact and this makes the person happier. The same can be said for people who run marathons, go skydiving, ride motorcycles, eat Brussels sprouts, go vegan, etc. They engage in those activities because they perceive they are getting some benefits from the behavior or activity. This is another way of saying they do it because they perceive it will make them happier.

While it's easy for people to see positive activities, behaviors, and habits as being happiness driven, it's far more difficult to see activities, behaviors, and habits that are costly, irrational, or risky as being done in the pursuit of happiness. They think the person making those choices must be sick, dysfunctional, or inherently immoral.

Often in hindsight, it is true that many people don't prefer the results of their heavy substance use. The outcomes can be costly monetarily, legally, mentally, emotionally, socially, and physically. With experience, these costs become predictable, and people often do contemplate them before they choose that next drink or hit. As borne out by the data, most heavy substance users make adjustments to their substance use as they come to believe they can be happier doing so, but there are those who don't make a change when others feel they should. The prevailing thought is that no one would freely choose such destructive behaviors. This is the argument we hear most often in favor of the idea that there is a state of involuntary behavior called addiction.

It's time we thoroughly break down that argument and challenge it. What it's really saying is that if a behavior or choice is extremely costly, then it must be involuntary. Another way of saying this is that it's impossible to make an irrational choice, so that if a behavior turns out to be irrational, then it must have been compelled, rather than freely chosen. When stated this way, you can see how absurd it is.

First, to be rational, that is to think through your potential options logically and determine which one will bring about the best results, takes effort and, in some cases, an enormous amount of effort. All people, addicts and non-addicts alike, fail at this task frequently! Plants and animals have it easy. They don't have to think things through to survive and thrive, but people do. Life is full of irrational decisions and the challenge is to continually gain knowledge and wisdom to make better and more "rational" decisions throughout life. When people cite irrationality as proof that a behavior is involuntary, are they really saying that it's impossible for humans to freely make irrational choices? The truth is that irrationality isn't proof of disease; it's proof of humanity.

Second, and more importantly, it's not odd for people to pay a high price for the things and activities they believe will make them happy. You don't need to look far for examples of this in everyday life. The Freedom Model co-author Steven Slate uses the following example to make this point: consider the costs of owning a big house. Obviously larger houses have a higher monetary price, but the higher costs don't stop there. They have higher property taxes and cost more to heat and air condition. The time as well as physical and mental energy expended to maintain a larger home are massive. It takes enormous effort to keep up extra rooms, such as a den, media room, finished basement, extra bedroom, home office, laundry room, and so on.

Contrast this with a modest apartment. Instead of a big 30-year mortgage, you could pay a smaller monthly rent. There is no property tax, no lawn and landscaping for you to maintain, no gutters to be cleaned, and no extra rooms to decorate, furnish, and keep clean. If something goes wrong structurally or with the plumbing or HVAC system, or the paint starts to peel, you don't have to worry about getting it fixed. You don't have to make any decisions about hiring help, contractors, or repairmen. Your landlord handles all these issues and the costs are already figured into your monthly rent. You needn't spend much time, effort, or mental energy on these things. Furthermore, you have no insurance or liability to worry about if someone slips on your steps and decides to sue, or some other unforeseen event happens on the periphery of the property. What's more, you don't have to worry about property values decreasing or the housing market softening and having your home become worth less than you paid for it. You take no such risks by renting. It's simply much easier being an apartment dweller, yet millions of people set a goal of buying a home and follow through on it every day.

If society looked at the homeownership versus renting a modest apartment situation in the same way it views heavy substance use, then everyone would say the homeowner is sick, diseased, disordered, or dysfunctional. Everyone would say that homeowners must have been traumatized so that now they are self-destructive and self-sabotaging. Everyone would say homeowners must have underlying issues of stress, anxiety, and depression that cause them to seek comfort in the immediate gratifications of living in a big home.

Of course, this analysis would be ridiculous. Some people like to rent small apartments while some people like to own big, luxurious mansions and there's a whole range of options that people prefer between those two choices. Everyone sees benefits in these various options that make one look better than the others, resulting in the desire for such a home and the willingness to pay the associated costs. People see things they believe they need to make them happy in a home, and then they pursue the home that they think meets their needs. They may wish the costs were lower to get the benefits they want, but nevertheless, they freely and willingly pay the price to get what they prefer.

People's preferences for substance use are no different. They have their own perspective on the benefits of substance use, and they will pay whatever the price is to get those benefits, if they think it is the option that best serves them. The PDP is how we sum up this fact. People take actions to achieve happiness, and they do so according to their own unique perspective. If you are putting effort into something, it's because you see it as the best available and viable option to achieve/sustain a happy existence. If your loved one truly didn't want to do something, then he wouldn't do it. All people are driven to always pursue happiness. (The preceding example was taken from *The Freedom Model for Addictions*, Chapter 7 "The Positive Drive Principle".)

ADDICTION INVOLVES HABIT

Addiction, with respect to alcohol and drug use, is associated with repetitive behavior. A thought or behavior that is repeated and practiced enough becomes second nature, or habitual, and requires little or no thought at all to do. That is why a crack user may go to the crack house every Friday after getting paid, but later claims he doesn't remember making the choice to use. People become so comfortable with a habitual behavior that they may keep doing it, in spite of negative consequences and unpleasant experiences because it provides comfort to them (a form of happiness). Because people continue doing their habit doesn't mean they can't stop, it just means they haven't stopped. Ponder this for a moment: if people who are "addicted" were actually powerless over alcohol and/or drugs, then they would never stop using – not when they ran out of money, not when they have to go to court, not while in a treatment program… not ever for any reason.

Have you ever wondered why the idea of "addiction as a disease" only includes behaviors and habits that society deems as negative? Habitual activities that are positive or neutral would never be labeled a disease. Driving a car is a habit which most adults do every day, yet no one would ever say we are suffering from the "addiction disease" of driving. Many people, including me, love reading and do it often. Sometimes I will stay up very late to finish a book and can be tired and irritable the next day. Does that mean I am "addicted" to reading and am therefore unable to stop? After all, I do overindulge from time to time in spite of the negative consequences of sleepiness, irritability, and inability to concentrate the next day.

What activity or activities do you really enjoy? Of those activities, think of a time when you have chosen to overindulge in spite of negative consequences. Really analyze in your mind one or two of those experiences and think about why you chose to do it, regardless of the potential, and sometimes predictable, unpleasant consequences. What you have just envisioned is the essence of addiction. Your loved one, who seems so out of control, who has made what you consider to be poor choices, and who has experienced dreadful consequences due to heavy drug and alcohol use, is making the exact same kinds of decisions you have made, engaging in something she likes, despite the likelihood of negative consequences. Simply because you and I cannot imagine why she wants to live that way does not mean that she has lost control or that her substance use is involuntary. What it means is you and I would not choose to live that way, but the fact is she does.

The disease theory of addiction is based on this kind of egocentric, moral judgment. People, including health professionals, look at those who have experienced negative consequences as a result of heavy alcohol and drug use, gambling, playing video games, watching pornography, shopping, or overeating, and conclude their behavior cannot possibly be voluntary and freely chosen.

Billions of dollars have been spent and are still being spent trying to discover the point at which people lose the power of personal choice with respect to certain behaviors, but as you look at peer-reviewed research, the studies supporting the disease theory all have a caveat or flaw that renders them inconsequential or inconclusive. Additionally, those studies are all funded by the pharmaceutical industry and/or state and federal governments who stand to collect billions from keeping addiction a disease.

Even those studies that claim to find a genetic marker or linkage for addiction fail to account for choice. Having a genetic predisposition or a genetic marker for a specific characteristic never replaces free will and choice. While the information may be interesting for the purposes of analysis, it can also discourage a healthy belief system and become a self-fulfilling prophecy.

BELIEFS DICTATE BEHAVIOR

Many family members may try to steer clear of the addiction disease debate. They say it is merely a matter of semantics, but how we use language shapes our cultural and personal beliefs. For example, consider hearing one of the following statements from a physician about your son: "He seems to have a drinking problem" or "He has alcoholism." These two statements evoke two totally different reactions. If you have noticed your son getting into some trouble due to his drinking, then you might agree with the first statement and wonder what you can do to help him get through this phase.

Reactions to the second statement are much more pronounced and urgent. You've just been told your son has what you may believe to be an incurable disease over which you and he have no control, and you feel hopeless and helpless. You may be embarrassed and blame a relative for passing down the dreaded, theoretical alcoholism gene. You may become overwhelmed with feelings of guilt, shame, remorse, anxiety, and anger.

Research where those diagnosed as alcoholics were given a test to gauge how strongly they believed in several common tenets of addiction (as a disease), such as "loss of control" or genetic predisposition to alcoholism showed that those who believe in these ideas most strongly were more likely to relapse following treatment. In fact, this belief system was one the top predictors of relapse after controlling for dozens of other factors (Miller, et. al., 1996). (For more information and research, see *The Freedom Model for Addictions*, Chapter 1.)

According to the book, *Alcoholics Anonymous*, the "bible" for 12-Step programs, the first step is to admit powerlessness over alcohol. The AA program, which is the basis for addiction treatment, recommends taking the first step daily. Imagine your first thought each day being, "I am powerless". How can this repetitive negative thinking bring about anything positive? For many, this powerlessness mantra leads to higher rates of dangerous binge drinking as well as mental health problems. Teaching people they are powerless over substances and are suffering from a disease from which they can never recover is a recipe for a lifetime of misery and struggle. And what makes it that much worse is – it is entirely false.

By providing people the truth—that all people are incredibly powerful because they have complete control over their thoughts and behaviors—then showing them exactly how they can change, they become free to think, feel, behave, and live however they choose. The truth is each one of us is responsible for our own happiness and success and always has been. Research has found that those who are successful, embrace this reality, and those who are not, reject it. Either way, both groups are still making a choice.

THE MYTH OF LOSS OF CONTROL

(*This section is an excerpt taken from Appendix A of The Freedom Model for Addictions that has been edited and adapted for this book.*)

The best thing we could ever do is to completely remove the word "control" from discussions of problematic substance use altogether because it confuses the issue. Some family members come to us saying they agree that their loved one can choose and that addiction is not a disease, but then they refer to their loved one's drinking as "out of control" or "uncontrolled" and express a desire for us to show their loved one how to "regain control". This all implies that heavy substance users aren't choosing their level of substance use, and indeed, many of them do feel truly out of control and certainly appear that way to you. This confusion in thought and feeling comes from the fact that phrases such as "out of control" are used in two different senses.

You lose control of a car if the brakes and steering fail. You can try to pump the brake pedal and turn the steering wheel all you want, but the car continues moving in the direction it was going before those systems failed until it runs out of momentum or crashes into something. In this situation, you have literally lost control of where you are going. It doesn't matter what you want to do. It doesn't matter whether you see another street you'd like to turn down or a place you'd like to park and get out. The car lands wherever it's fated to land, and you have no further say in the matter. For those who've had this experience, it is truly terrifying.

Addiction theorists are fond of saying that "addicts can't put on the brakes", directly comparing substance users to cars, evoking the situation mentioned above. They mention various systems and regions in the brain and claim to know that these areas are broken, just like a car that won't stop. Choice is not possible in this model, just like the driver of the car with no brakes could not choose to stop the car. This is the sense in which most people say that addicts and alcoholics are "out of control."

However, the evidence we reviewed shows that this isn't the case at all. When addicts or alcoholics see another path they'd rather take, they steer their way there. I'm certain if you think back on your loved one's history, you have witnessed this exact behavior from this person you may believe is "out of control." When they don't feel like going farther down the road of substance use, they hit the brakes (or, more accurately, they stop hitting the gas). This happens on a situational level when people decide to bring an end to a drinking/drugging session, and it happens on a whole-life level when people quit or dramatically adjust their substance use, either temporarily or for good, as the epidemiological evidence on "recovery" rates proves (see *The Freedom Model for Addictions* Chapter 1). So the idea of being out of control is patently false and should not be used nor should the idea of "regaining control." You can't regain what was never lost. You can't regain control of your uncontrollable car by offering it money, yet "out of control" substance users can be persuaded to "control" their substance use with monetary offers, both in and outside the laboratory.

There is another, non-literal sense in which "out of control" is used, and it gets mixed up with the one we just discussed, leading to much confusion. If a young child at a park starts misbehaving by swearing, name-calling, hitting other children, and repeatedly refusing to obey his mother's demands to stop this behavior, we say that child is "out of control". He is flouting the attempts of his mother to control him. He's flouting the subtle attempts that other parents make to control him through menacing looks. He's flouting what he already knows are standards of behavior he's expected to follow. He is in full control of himself in those moments. He is doing exactly what he wants to do, but it is clearly not what others want him to do.

When we say the child is "out of control", what we really mean is that he's out of social control. He is behaving contrary to the standards he's expected to live by in his social environment. He refuses to obey social norms and the desires and commands of others. He isn't doing what society deems he "should" do.

This latter sense of the phrase "out of control" more accurately describes problematic substance use than the literal sense of the phrase. "Uncontrolled" substance use is simply that which breaks accepted norms of behavior. If a college student gets falling-down drunk at a keg party, we don't suggest that he isn't freely choosing to do it because that is acceptable behavior from a college student in our culture. We might say those kids at the kegger are "out of control", but we don't mean it literally—we just mean that they're acting wildly. However, if a 40-year-old mother of two gets falling-down drunk at a party in front of the wrong people, we say she's literally "out of control", and she may be shipped off to a rehab in short order. The dividing line is the fact that our culture says 40-year-old mothers shouldn't behave this way but college students can and should. We say that the college kids are "out of control", and the 40-year-old is "out of control". But the same phrase means different things when applied to these different people and situations.

People whose substance use is described as "uncontrolled" or "out of control" are using in a way that is socially unacceptable. They are still in full control of themselves and their behaviors. The meaning of the phrase is switched so that people can treat them like children while pretending they are not. When we say a child is "out of control", we all know what that means and what the remedy is. They aren't behaving as we, their superiors, demand they should behave, and bringing them under control means disciplining them, scaring them into following demands of how they should behave. This coercion makes children angry, but they are forced to accept it because of their subservient status as children.

Adults, on the other hand, have a different status in our culture. Adults are supposed to be free and independent to do whatever they like, if it doesn't directly harm others. With respect to substance use, loved ones and treatment professionals can't be as direct about chastising substance users for their behaviors, telling them that they know better than the substance users, nor can they say that substance users must follow their orders and direction as they show them how they should live their lives. This attempt to control and direct another adult's freely chosen behaviors creates a thousand times the opposition that it does in children.

None of us want to be told how to live as adults, and we rebel against it at all costs. Therefore, it is thought that the commands by those who know better must be subtle and disguised to be effective. The claim that someone's drinking or drugging is "out of control" is thus used in the literal sense with adults (and some adolescents who've matured to a level of intellectual independence) to cover up the coercive dynamic. That is, what's really going on is that the substance users' freely chosen, fully controlled substance use goes against the wishes of others and those others are demanding they stop it. The demand/coercion is reframed as an offer of help, a diagnosis of the "loss of control" and "treatment for the disease of addiction." It is said to be a way to help the substance users "regain control" that they've literally lost because of their own behavior. It's all a ruse and a giant cultural charade. It allows the coercers to hide their coercion and the substance users to submit to the coercion while saving face and not appearing to be lower status individuals who are being bullied into living their lives on terms set by others.

Of course, it doesn't usually work so smoothly because, whether you believe it or not, substance users, by and large, inherently know they are doing what they want to do, and that their substance use isn't involuntary, even though the results may be troubling. When substance users argue with the suggestion that they are literally "out of control", they are then said to be "in denial", which is just another symptom of the disease—this symptom, "denial", is said to hide from the substance user the truth that he is truly out of control! When faced with the "denial diagnosis", substance users have a second chance to acquiesce by "realizing" that they're "in denial" and then "admitting" that they cannot control their substance use. This is usually when they begin to realize there are benefits to participating in the charade.

The substance user and you, the loved one who is trying to help, both get to decide whether or not you will participate in the loss of control, disease charade. For both of you, there seem to be benefits to participating. For the substance user, by taking on the addict/alcoholic identity, especially when it is new, much of their past and current behaviors are excused, and they hope their future behaviors will be excused as well. Even though the substance user may be facing jail time, they are afforded the opportunity to go into treatment instead of jail, in some cases multiple times. Most people won't pass up a "get out of jail free" card. Many employers will help a fair to good employee find treatment and hold their job for them, and many loved ones will excuse violence, adultery, and generally offensive behaviors as symptoms of a disease and give chance after chance for the individual to get help and hopefully change.

For the families and loved ones of the substance user, there are benefits to playing the charade too, at least initially. For parents, it may be easier to accept that your son or daughter is not freely choosing their heavy substance use. While many parents will initially question what they did wrong that made their adult child have such problems, they may find comfort in the notion that addiction is a disease that can strike anyone at any time, much like cancer. If it's due to genetics, then perhaps it was predetermined, and thus nothing the parents could have done would have stopped it. For spouses and partners, there is some limited comfort in believing that the spouse is sick and diseased and therefore not actually choosing substance use over the relationship.

In the end, many of these benefits that loved ones experience have a limited life span. Eventually, as the family and loved ones invest in sending the substance user to treatment programs and partaking in treatment themselves that is directed toward them, the relationship with the substance user usually breaks down as the family gets weary of participating in the charade and of investing in the relationship with so little return.

That is when you get overly emotional exchanges and families implementing "tough love". These tactics are very telling with respect to the erroneous disease model. Can you imagine screaming at your son who has cancer that you're done with him and his behavior, and that you can no longer support him due to his cancer? And can you imagine oncologists advocating that families cut off their loved one with cancer? No one would ever do that, yet it happens in households around the country every day regarding "addiction".

When everyone buys into the disease charade, that is when things can take a turn for the worse, and the future becomes most bleak for everyone involved. As substance users go in and out of support group meetings, treatment, and addiction therapies, many begin to take on the powerless belief system fully, and then all bets are off. What they once felt was a behavior they engaged in willingly because they wanted to do it, becomes something that is mysterious and confusing to them. They know that they shouldn't like their substance use, according to cultural norms, and in some cases, they actually convince themselves that they don't like it and never did. When we engage in a behavior that we think we don't like and believe we have no control to stop it, that is seriously problematic.

I talked with a 35 year old woman recently who is literally drinking herself to death. She has been to rehab a few times and has tried 12 Step meetings on and off for several years but said she doesn't like them and doesn't buy into the idea that she has a disease.

However, when I asked her why she thinks that she keeps drinking, and what benefits she believes she's getting from using alcohol, she got upset with me and said, "I hate it! It does nothing for me! But I keep doing it. It's killing me and I just keep doing it. I can't stop!" This complete confusion makes it virtually impossible for me or anyone to help her.

12 Step programs, and addiction treatment based on it, have muddied the waters to such an extreme that, in some cases, people are actually drinking and drugging themselves to death, believing they are compelled to do it and that they are physically unable to stop. They truly believe they don't like anything about it and don't want to do it, and they have no idea why they continue it.

Imagine repeatedly hitting yourself in the head with a hammer, not knowing why you're doing it, and feeling as if you can't stop. Nobody would ever do that, right? You think it's absurd and know that no one would ever do it because there is no benefit to be gained from such an action – but now let's consider substance use. On the one hand, it can certainly cause physical harm and negative consequences, but, on the other hand, there are definitely benefits to using or no one would ever do it. Can't we all agree that ingesting substances is not equal to hitting yourself in the head with a hammer? More than half the adults in this country drink alcohol at some level and more than 20% admit to using drugs for recreational purposes at some point in their lives, so unlike hitting yourself in the head with a hammer which no one does, the act of drinking and taking drugs is desirable to a great many people.

Even the treatment community itself acknowledges some

perceived benefits to substance use when they say that people use substances to "self-medicate" and that the effects of some substances are so wonderful that people are hooked from just one hit (which is not supported by the data). So now we have generations of people struggling with substance use who are told they shouldn't like it. They are told they can't possibly like it so much that they would keep doing it after experiencing negative consequences. They are told that because they keep using after experiencing negative consequences that they must be mentally ill or deranged. They are told that they are morally and spiritually bankrupt, self-centered, narcissistic, egotistical, and suffering from defects of character and that the only way they can stop using is through ongoing therapy, medications, prayer, and meetings. They are told they must have experienced trauma, stress, a bad childhood, or that they have mental health issues that have led to their substance use and they are told that it is in their genes. They are given a whole host of excuses for their substance use, none of which include the simple idea that perhaps, there is something about it they actually like.

The only way people effectively change their behaviors is by honestly assessing the personal value of the behavior to them and deciding if they can be happier making some adjustment. They must be able to identify what benefits they perceive they are getting from substance use and this is far more important than recognizing the costs.

Most heavy substance users are not honest when assessing these benefits for fear of receiving harsh judgment from their loved ones and those in the recovery community, and some have truly lost sight of them. This makes it virtually impossible for them to make a lasting change as their attempts to change become solely based on avoiding the costs and consequences, while still maintaining a preference for heavy substance use that they won't acknowledge or no longer recognize.

THE PROBLEM WITH COERCED TREATMENT

The substance users forced into treatment have traditionally made up only 10% to 20% of those who fit formal diagnoses for addictions/ substance use disorders. They've been misled into believing they can't control themselves. They've been coerced into playing the charade. And then the results, ongoing struggle, "relapse", and requiring ongoing support, treatment, and aftercare confirm in their minds the addiction disease model of problematic substance use as they then attest to it.

Those coerced into abstinence struggle more because they haven't been allowed to make their own decisions. They "need support" not to battle addiction, because addiction doesn't exist, but rather they need support to deal with the fact that they're being coerced to quit substance use when they really want to continue it. Their "support systems" don't magically transfer strength into them, which then helps them to remain abstinent. Instead, the people in these systems are more like supporting players in a film that help to make the whole scene more believable. Their life has become about playing this charade of being addicted and battling addiction (i.e., liking substance use and being deprived of it because of coercive involvements).

For those who do experience a time of abstinence, they, exactly like the self-changers, have decided during that period not using is more beneficial to them than using. Many become the memoirists, the activists, the counselors, and the general spokespeople for the charade of addiction and recovery. Sadly, many "addicts turned helpers/experts" continue to struggle throughout their lives because they truly believe in the "loss of control" myth and continuously reinforce it in their own lives. The other 80% to 90% are the self-changers, those who avoid the system and stay silent, unnoticed, and unresearched (for the most part), and most of them have no subsequent struggles with substance use. They simply move on.

Those who face coercion are put in a situation where it's not worth arguing with this model. If they say they're free, they're sanctioned for it. If they agree to loss of control, they're granted some leeway. Agreeing to speak of their substance use as an "out of control" behavior has benefits for heavy substance users. They can then "lose control" and "relapse" occasionally if they explain it this way (that is, they get a pass to occasionally do what they want instead of what others demand).

The myth of "loss of control" helps those who work in treatment do their jobs and serve their real customers, who are, in most cases, not the clients/patients themselves, but rather their loved ones, employers, or law enforcement agencies. Those parties want to buy abstinence for their loved one and treatment providers sell it. This isn't a cynical view; it's a historical and an economic fact that has incentivized the treatment industry to function in a way that satisfies those parties. These entities don't exist to empower problematic substance users to discover their most rewarding choices. They exist to manipulate them into abstinence. So the recovery society and treatment providers present a false alternative designed to corner substance users into choosing abstinence—either you abstain or you go out of control using substances to disastrous ends. To make their false alternative real, they created family programs in which loved ones are trained to make disastrous consequences come down on the substance user with "tough love." These methods are designed to make the choice to abstain for the substance user a no-brainer. They don't want substance users to think about their options at all; they just want them to accept their (the helpers') conclusions of what they (the substance users) should do. (*For a more thorough discussion, see Chapters 8 and 9 of The Freedom Model for Addictions.*)

To answer the initial question, what is addiction? Addiction, as you know it, does not exist. Addiction is not a disease, and, in fact, no one is ever powerless over their behaviors. The same can be said for alcoholism. People engage in behaviors they think will make them happy, and, in some cases, they engage in those behaviors frequently and heavily, which can create a habit. All people have the innate ability to change their habits and do so throughout their lives.

CHAPTER 3:

DENIAL, CO-DEPENDENCY, AND ENABLING: HARMFUL, INACCURATE LABELS

Whether they have had personal experience with a substance use problem or not, most people are familiar with the concepts of denial, co-dependency, and enabling as these terms have entered the mainstream over the past century. Those who have been dealing with a substance user for any length of time may have been told that they or their loved one were in denial or that they are enablers or are co-dependent. These labels are not only inaccurate but they do nothing to help the substance user or the family. Instead, they systematically shift the responsibility for the substance user's problematic behavior to those around him, who are the very people who truly are powerless over his actions.

44

DENIAL

The theory of denial was first identified by Dr. Sigmund Freud to describe how an individual rejects something they find too uncomfortable to accept, such as the death of a loved one, a terminal illness, or a traumatic experience. More recently the denial theory has been used by the treatment industry to ensure even those who reject the idea they have the addiction disease, or what is now known as substance use disorder (SUD), can be coerced into treatment.

While it is understandable a person may go through a period of denial when facing the death of a child or his own terminal illness, there is no data to support the idea that people are unaware of their behaviors or of the consequences of their behaviors. As substance use requires prior thought, planning, and action, like all behaviors, the idea that a person is unaware they are partaking in the behavior is completely absurd.

Behaviors we do repeatedly may become nearly automatic, but this does not mean they do not require prior thought. It means we process the thought more rapidly than other behaviors. So, if denial is not referring to a person being unaware of the behavior, then what is a substance user denying? Treatment professionals say substance users in denial are unaware of the problems their substance use has caused them and others. They also say those in denial, deny they are addicted and powerless to stop on their own. How convenient for treatment professionals: those in denial of their addiction need treatment services, especially if they believe they are not addicted and can stop on their own.

I would like to ask you an important question about the concept of denial with respect to substance use: do you think it is more advantageous for your loved one to believe he has the power and ability to stop his substance use or to believe that he does not have the power and ability to stop it? Logically speaking, of course, it would be more advantageous for people to believe they do have the power to stop. As a matter of fact, this belief is crucial for anyone seeking to make a change in their substance use habits.

Denial, with respect to addiction, is nothing more than a disagreement. A heavy substance user is disagreeing that he/she is addicted and therefore incapable of stopping or moderating substance use. Denial is actually the substance user telling people the truth, that he (the substance user) is in control and doing exactly what he wants to do. The problem is his truth is completely dismissed, and instead treatment providers and "helpers" label this disagreement as a "symptom" of the "addiction disease" and use it to gain control over him.

It's just another case of circular logic that is intended to force people into doing things they don't truly want to do. It's bypassing the crucial steps of providing factual information and allowing the substance users to come up with their own conclusions on what they feel is best for them.

CO-DEPENDENCY

In much the same way, the theory of co-dependency allows treatment providers to also label the family as "sick" and in need of treatment. Initially, co-dependency was created to explain the often volatile relationships between heavy substance users and their loved ones. The co-dependency theory makes two false assumptions. The first false assumption is the substance user is sick and suffering from a disease, which they are not. The second false assumption is if someone stays in a relationship with the substance user, he or she is also sick and in need of treatment. Both assumptions involve illnesses that take the place of individual responsibility for thoughts, behaviors, choices, and actions. In reality, both the substance user and loved one are making their own choices based on their desires and perceived needs at any given moment. They are certainly not suffering from an illness.

Family members and friends of substance users seeking the help of addiction professionals are vulnerable. They may feel immense guilt, shame, frustration, anxiety, and confusion. They are desperate to find a solution to their problems and will grasp at anything that gives them some perception of control over the situation. This is why ideas of co-dependency and enabling are even palatable to them. Family members may think, "Perhaps this is partially my fault; I can control myself and then, in turn, control the substance user through changing my behavior." This idea then gave rise to the concepts of "tough love", addiction as a family illness, and family addiction therapy. Unfortunately, these ideas have done little to help families or substance users over the past 50 years and, in some cases, have done real damage to already strained family relationships.

The problem with these ideas is, like the theories of "denial" and "addiction", they assume people are unaware of their motives, thoughts, choices, and behaviors. People remain in relationships with substance users for much the same reason substance users continue to use substances, because they are seeking happiness, however fleeting it may be.

Those trying to help families with alcohol or drug problems must understand that people do things they believe will satisfy them or make them happy. The active substance user wants to get high or drunk. Friends and family members stay involved with the substance user, regardless of the chaotic and sometimes abusive behavior that comes with it, because they believe they can be happier doing so than they can be not doing it. Because these relationships often cause both participants pain and unhappiness, they are classified by the treatment industry as unhealthy, sick relationships. Unhappiness, drama, and personal pain, however, are normal consequences of certain choices, not a sickness. They are also normal parts of the human experience.

ENABLING

Can you kill someone with kindness? Can you harm a person by giving them money, food, shelter, gifts, or affection? The alcohol and drug treatment industry, 12-Step programs, and addiction professionals all say, yes, you can. They call this "killing with kindness" enabling, and this label quite literally blames parents, spouses, friends, and loved ones for an individual's drug or alcohol use. Not only is this idea completely illogical, it demonstrates why drug treatment fails so many people.

Let's look at an example. John was convicted of DWI and, as part of his sentence, he is forced by the courts to attend treatment and abstain from drinking for a period of one year. But on Christmas, a well-meaning friend gives him a bottle of expensive wine. To celebrate, John and his wife make a nice dinner at home and enjoy a couple of glasses of wine each. By treatment and the court's standards, John has relapsed. Is John's friend to blame for him drinking the wine? What about his wife who shared a romantic dinner with him?

The only person responsible for John drinking the wine is John. If my employer lays me off, my spouse cheats, or my son gets arrested, and I drink and drive and injure someone in an accident, the responsibility for that series of choices and their consequences are all mine. I own them. I may have used one of those events as a reason to drink, but that was my choice too. My drinking is not the fault of my employer, my spouse, or my son. Therefore, just as the choices and actions of others have no bearing on John's choice to drink, neither does the continued help of his family and friends.

Parents often call and ask, "What can we do? We keep bailing our son out of jail, paying his bills, and taking him in when he says he wants help, but he only lasts a few days or weeks and then he's off and running again. We don't want him to die, but we don't know what else to do!" The answer resides in the intent of the help that is given. Most people believe they are helping their loved one for their loved one's benefit and that is not entirely true. They are actually providing that help for themselves, which is a valid reason.

When we encounter difficult situations over which we have no control, it is human nature to do everything within our power to exert some influence or control over it. Family members bail their loved one out of jail, hire attorneys, take in the substance user one more time, and pay their bills because they hope this time will be the time their loved one will finally change, and then they (the parents, sibling, friend, or spouse) will finally be able to relax and be happy. While most heavy substance users do change eventually, some do not, leaving their family and friends bitter, worn out, and quickly losing hope.

Then there are those who make the difficult decision to cut the substance user off. They say, "You are an adult, if this is the way you choose to live your life, you are on your own. I'm done." Whether you believe it or not, for these families, the risk of their loved one ending up in jail or dying is exactly the same as for those family members who continue to provide everything. This is because what you do or don't do has little, if any, influence on what the substance user does or does not do.

What you decide to do for a loved one struggling with substance use problems is irrelevant as to whether or not they will continue using substances. Once all the misinformation about addiction, codependency, enabling, and denial are stripped away, families are left with this reality: the only person you can control is you. No one is sick. No one is powerless; not the substance user, not the family members, not their friends, no one. Substance users not only choose to use substances because they want to, they also do this knowing full well the risks and costs they will incur, whether they admit that to you or not.

When contemplating what you should or should not do for the substance user when they ask for help, it is important to know your motives and employ some common sense. If you give the substance user money, regardless of what he says he will do with it, you are providing a resource for him to purchase substances. Even if you pay his bills directly, you are still freeing up money for the substance user to get drugs and/or alcohol, but you are also ensuring he has a warm place to sleep. The point is there is no right or wrong answer. The decision should be based on what you want for you – not what you hope the substance user will do if you give him what he wants or don't give him what he wants.

No one wants to lose a child, spouse, parent, relative, or friend to substance use. We all want to see our loved ones become happy and prosperous in life. When it comes right down to it, the most effective way to help someone achieve that lifestyle is to achieve it for yourself.

CHAPTER 4:

WHY DO PEOPLE DEVELOP SUBSTANCE USE PROBLEMS? BREAKING LEARNED CONNECTIONS

While many who enroll in *The Freedom Model for Addictions* at our Retreats have led relatively normal, or even charmed lives in many respects, there is a misperception that substance use problems are a result of past trauma, mental health issues, or are a response to profound difficulties or stress in life. While some guests have experienced past or current financial difficulties, relationship issues, or even abuse or traumatic loss, many admit their substance use problems started long before those events or challenges. Some will admit their substance use caused their current problems and then go on to say they used more because of those problems, further compounding them. It can become a vicious cycle.

The problem with saying that stress is a cause for substance use is that life stressors will not go away after someone completes *The Freedom Model for Addictions* or any treatment program. As a matter of fact, the stress level is likely to increase temporarily as the individual actively works to rebuild his life. Believing a person must be shielded from stress or he will drink or drug again is a losing proposition. Stress is inevitable and it provides a ready-made excuse: "Life is just too tough. I am going to go get high."

Shielding the individual from life's stresses has become the mission of the treatment industry. By convincing people they are fragile victims of circumstance, the treatment industry has effectively created a pool of ever-deteriorating, powerless people who serve as a constant source of revenue for the treatment industry. This learned connection between stress and substance use is genius in a terribly destructive way. Life stressors are unavoidable, thus all treatment is devoted to shielding an individual from the unavoidable. This ensures "relapse" is inevitable since the two remain forever connected— relapse comes after stress. With continued use comes more treatment and 12-Step meetings. And so it goes.

The good news is there is an escape from learned connections; they can be broken. You and your loved one do not have to believe this destructive and false connection between negative life circumstances and "relapse". You and your loved one are free, strong beings, and now you, and everyone in your sphere of influence, can start acting on this truth. You can break the connection and address stress, trauma, and substance use as individual issues, and this will enable you to tackle each issue separately and more easily.

When you think about the stress/trauma/substance use connection, envision a large rubber band ball. Substance users enter treatment and are told that their substance use is caused by a number of external factors outside the simple decision/desire to use substances. Well meaning therapists and counselors explore childhood trauma, abuse, relationship and financial difficulties, life stressors, emotional and health problems, etc., and say those things are causing the substance user to use substances. This means that individual must solve all of those problems prior to being able to stop using, right? Yet, the substance user is then told by that same addiction professional that they must first stop their substance use to be able to address those other problems. But how is that possible if those problems cause substance use? As you can imagine, this creates frustration and confusion. Where does one problem start and the other end? Thus what you have is a massive rubber band ball that can't possibly be unraveled. The only way to tackle it will be to take it apart, one piece at a time, and when you do that, you see the rubber bands are actually not connected at all, they only appeared that way at first glance.

The truth is all people experience stress, trauma, and difficulties in life. ALL PEOPLE. And the vast majority don't use substances heavily, and many don't use them at all. This reality proves the direct causation theory to be wrong. However, there is a belief within our culture that substances have the power to relax you and ease stress at least temporarily. With these beliefs it is reasonable to assume that many people use stress, trauma, and difficulties as a reason to use substances, but that's far different than a cause.

IF STRESS AND HARDSHIP ARE NOT THE CAUSE, THEN WHAT IS?

There is a fundamental difference between a cause and a reason. A cause for a reaction is an involuntary process, such as flinching at a sudden, loud sound. It is clear the choice to use substances, like all other choices in life, is completely voluntary. As a matter of fact, we know any choice we make has a foundation of thought and reasoning behind it. Stress cannot cause drinking, but stress can certainly be considered a reason to drink. People reason their way from stress to substance use all the time. "Cause" is a term that mainly applies to inanimate objects, but the term "reason" accounts for the presence of the human mind and its role in behavior.

There are infinite reasons for the choices we make. But underneath the details of all of them is a consistent desire for greater happiness and life satisfaction. As discussed previously, the Positive Drive Principle states that all humans always move in the direction they believe will make them happy. Whatever the situation and circumstances your loved one has experienced, they have always been in control, and they have always used free will to search for happiness. Within the Freedom Model curriculum and exercises, our readers learn that there are no causes for substance use, but rather, reasoning through free will, choice, and the desire for happiness that motivates the choice.

When interviewed by researchers, what predicted long-term success for those who completed The Freedom Model at the Retreats, and our previous program iterations of the Saint Jude Program, was one thing: embracing and accepting personal responsibility. Successful graduates began to see themselves as capable of change and responsible for their future and they set about pursuing personal happiness. Their positive changes had nothing to do with ongoing support group meeting attendance, claiming to be powerless, or being shielded from stress. Rather, their success was based on a cognitive shift towards embracing their immense freeing power of choice and their desire for greater happiness in their lives. These were, and continue to be, the common denominators for success, and remain the underpinnings of the educational exercises in The Freedom Model.

If your loved one can see themselves as free to choose, they will realize that "addiction" cannot be. If they embrace their free will and the simple fact that they are the culmination of their choices, they will already be halfway down the path to a more fulfilling life. If you and your loved one fully comprehend there is no cause for using substances, but rather, people create many reasons for using, then you will feel in control over your respective lives permanently.

CHAPTER 5:

PEOPLE CAN AND DO CHANGE

(This section is an excerpt taken from Chapter 16 of The Freedom Model for Addictions that has been edited and adapted for this book.)

When your loved one stops approaching their substance use as a matter of "battling addiction," they're left with the fact that they have a strong desire to use substances. Throughout The Freedom Model, we call this their preference for substance use. Your loved one, like you, can change a preference, and can stop wanting to use substances to the same degree that he has in the past. It starts and ends with changing the way he thinks about his options.

The Oxford Dictionary defines "preference" as "the fact of liking or wanting one thing more than another". The first thing to know about preferences is that to prefer anything is to think it's a better option than some other options you have. A preference isn't based on what you think about something in isolation; it's based on how you think it stacks up in comparison to other things. This point cannot be stressed enough: people do not change a preference by looking at one option in isolation. They must include a comparison to other options. In the realm of substance use, this means that simply looking at the costs and benefits of a drug is not enough to make you not prefer it. People prefer some things over other things.

To make this point clearer, let's look at an example of owning a motorcycle. Let's say you are getting bored with your current motorcycle; you've had it for years, and it's been needing repairs lately. But you love that old machine; many memories of trips through the mountains were made on it, and you had some really good times. So you spend a day making a list of the costs versus the benefits of owning that bike. Still unsure of whether to sell it, days drag on as you compare the list. As time passes, you realize it's been a difficult decision about whether to keep the motorcycle. A week later, you go for a ride on the old machine and pass by a motorcycle dealership. You see the new models that came out that year. Suddenly, your bike looks and feels really dated in comparison. The many benefits of the newer bikes catch your fancy, and you drive home knowing you'll go back to the dealership to make the trade. What happened?

You preferred the benefits of the new bike to the benefits of the old one. This point is crucial: once you saw that new paint and chrome, the cost of owning the old machine wasn't a factor in your choosing to get the new bike. Think about that. The cost involved with owning "old reliable" was forgotten in the presence of new chrome and unscratched paint. What motivated the change was the bright new motorcycle sitting next to the old one, the choice was suddenly easy to make. What was once your dream bike 15 years ago, with all its bells and whistles, has become a comparably faded relic when sitting next to the new one. Simply stated, costs and benefits of a single option do not motivate people to change as effectively as when they add in the benefits of a comparable option. Here is why: a benefits-to-benefits analysis works because it uses a person's basis for motivation, the PDP, in the decision-making process. When change is motivated by a pursuit of happiness and comparing the benefits of various options, progress and change are the natural outcomes. In contrast, just comparing the costs versus the benefits of only one option will lead to indecision and staying with the old, known, comfortable option.

The idea of comparing the benefits of various options should not be confused with replacing substance use habits with something like a hobby, working out, or meetings. This replacement theory will be covered in detail later, but it needs to be said now so you don't misunderstand and encourage your loved one to go down that dead-end path. Replacing a substance use habit with anything else is ineffective because of the motive behind such replacements.

In the motorcycle analogy, the man chose the new bike for its benefits, not to distract himself from the old bike. In contrast in the replacement scenario, the intention is not primarily to seek the benefits of going to meetings or working out, but rather to distract yourself from doing what you like to do, which is to use substances heavily. Whenever people try to distract themselves from something, such as heavy substance use, they still prefer it and will eventually go back to it. Going back to it shows they still prefer it. So, as your loved one moves forward, it is important as a starting point that he be honest with himself about how much he still prefers substance use before seeking alternative, beneficial options. Replacements will fail if he still prefers to use heavily, whereas being motivated to seek the benefits of a new option and moving on from an old option naturally works.

The dominance of benefits in decision-making should be clear by now. Motivation comes from perceived benefits. Nevertheless, those who struggle with problematic substance use tend to focus primarily on costs to motivate them to change. What's more, they don't consider the benefits of alternatives (i.e. abstinence or moderation). This has likely been what your loved one has done in the past when he's tried to change. Please understand, we're not saying that costs don't matter or that they don't figure into the decision to change. However, they're not the prime motivator, so it's crucial that your loved one shift his attention toward the benefits of his options. The costs are merely a starting point from which people may then begin to question whether they have more beneficial options available to them.

Staring at the costs of use, which is the primary goal of treatment, will almost always make the high from a substance look more appealing, not less appealing. The PDP works on relative happiness values, not on costs. If a high from cocaine is fun to you, staring at a foreclosure notice that has been served to you because of your pricey habit is not going to make getting high on cocaine less appealing. It might for a moment—and then you will find yourself going to get coke again. This time the high you will get from the cocaine, when compared to the feelings associated with looking at the foreclosure notice, is a much better option. And it isn't even a close race; cocaine will always win until you develop a new option that you prefer. So again, costs are very temporary motivators, and without a new option to compare to the cocaine high, the old standby of cocaine (or other substance) will remain your loved one's go-to option.

We've now established two keys to preference change:

1. Focus on benefits.
2. Focus on the benefits of more than one option.

This is how *The Freedom Model for Addictions* shows people exactly how they can make a lasting preference change, as this is precisely how all people change.

UNHAPPINESS ISN'T A CAUSE OF HEAVY SUBSTANCE USE

With all our talk about heavy substance use being driven by the pursuit of happiness, there is a common misconception people have about *The Freedom Model for Addictions*. They think that we're saying depression or unhappiness causes heavy substance use. This is the most common learned connection. The next logical misconception is that the solution to heavy substance use is to get over unhappiness or depression first and then sobriety will follow. Let's be clear and firm about this: there is no data to support nor do we teach that heavy substance use is caused by unhappiness or relieved by happiness.

You can be genuinely unhappy or depressed and not feel the slightest need or desire for heavy substance use. In fact, 80% of people with mood disorders do not have substance use problems, and the minority who have both substance use problems and mood disorders, such as depression or bipolar, have no special difficulty getting over their substance use problems. Their rates of "recovery" are just as high as those who don't have these problems (Lopez-Quintero et al., 2011). Take a moment to let that sink in because it's contrary to our cultural belief.

No matter what your loved one's current level of happiness is—whether he's depressed or living in constant bliss—he will prefer heavy substance use if he sees it as his best path to happiness, and he will not prefer it if he does not see it as his best path to happiness. The solution to substance use problems is not to get happier first, but to cease to believe that heavy substance use is his best available option for acquiring happiness. Trying to resolve unhappiness first is indirect, and keeps heavy troubling use alive as a potential option for when unhappiness hits again. That learned connection is dangerous to believe. The substance user must carefully explore his substance use options with a focus on benefits for the most direct path to developing a lasting preference change that could eradicate any further attraction to troubling heavy substance use patterns. Furthermore, when he no longer feels dependent on heavy substance use and stops paying all its costs, he will regain many resources that he will be able to devote to building the happiest life possible.

THE PREFERENCE RUT

A preference for heavy substance use is usually built slowly over time. As heavy substance users begin to experience higher costs, they go in one of two directions: they seek to adjust their substance use in the hopes of finding greater happiness, or they feel badly about the high costs and, in some cases, play the victim while continuing to use in the same manner. Those who have kept the costly pattern going for a long time may feel intense anger and shame over the costs, and this can leave them in a serious rut. The guilt and shame becomes a reason for ongoing heavy substance use. They've likely forgotten what it's like to live without hating their choices. They may have forgotten what it's like to enjoy a moderate level of substance use that leaves them with no regrets, or they may not remember a time when they weren't nagged by those they love for their substance use. This has become a way of life for them, and as unpleasant as it is, the prospect of stopping or moderating their use is not enticing.

You likely remember a time in your loved one's life when he had plenty of fun and excitement without costly levels of substance use. He probably dealt with many life problems before without attaching them to heavy substance use. There was likely a time when he didn't have such a singular focus on one repetitious activity. But during the time he has been in the rut, bored with the repetition, tired from the nagging sense of need and dependence, hating the price he is paying for something that's lost its luster, he has forgotten that he really can have a happy and exciting life without this costly option. In The Freedom Model, we pose this question to our readers, "Are you ready to explore and rediscover your potential for greater happiness?" We let them know that we understand that the rut they now find themselves in is "safe" in some sense because it's predictable. We know that the longer and deeper people have been in the rut, the more they stand to gain and discover by peeking out of it and getting a fresh look at their substance use options.

What is taught in The Freedom Model is a means of assessing the personal value of each substance use option: heavy use, moderate use, and abstinence. We ask our readers if they are willing to believe in the possibility that adjusted use or abstinence holds more benefits than they previously thought it did. Then we ask if they are willing to question the benefits they think they get from heavy substance use.

Changing heavy substance use requires a change in personal preference. This is true for everyone. Whether people go through treatment and then change their substance use, or stop on their own, both do so because they've changed their preference. For the 5-20% that go to treatment and are successful, they make the change in spite of what they learn in treatment, not because of it. The Freedom Model Chapter 2 outlines how those people who are successful in treatment actually made the decision to change their substance use habit, often prior to going into treatment, which ultimately led to their success. In other words, they had already stopped their addiction. They went to treatment simply because they thought they needed it, then, when they are successful, they naturally attribute their success to the treatment they received. Unfortunately, as evidenced by the low success rates of treatment (lower than the rate for self-changers), there are many who succumb to what is being taught in treatment and although they had decided to stop prior to treatment, they begin to struggle post-treatment believing they must continuously fight the boogeyman that is addiction.

QUESTIONING DRUG EFFECTS

One way *The Freedom Model for Addictions* helps people to examine their preference for heavy substance use is by questioning the alleged benefits and effects they perceive they are getting from substance use. Alcohol and drugs are neither as good nor as bad as they are made out to be. People take for granted that drugs and alcohol have a set of miraculous effects, negative and positive, harmful and helpful. Some of these effects are the inevitable outcome of a substance's pharmacological action. However, some of these effects are either nonexistent or the product of nondrug factors. Since people's view of substances motivates their decisions to use them, Chapters 17-20 of The Freedom Model sorts through the various effects so the reader can understand which ones really come from the drugs and which ones don't. A changed view on the powers and effects of substances leads to a change in the motivation to use them.

In Chapter 17, The Freedom Model challenges some of the most deeply held views on the powers of substances. Please note, I am not saying substances have no effects at all—they most certainly do. Whenever we have this discussion, some people get annoyed and say "So you're saying drugs don't affect a person?!" Of course they do. What we're saying is that they don't affect people in the ways that are commonly believed and discussed.

Substances can physically stimulate or sedate our bodies, including altering heart rate, blood pressure, breathing, temperature, digestion, and neurotransmission. These things happen without question, and we needn't get into the finer details of all these effects. We acknowledge that these effects occur as a matter of pharmacology and that they play a part in the total experience of using substances. Succinctly, here is what we mean when we say that substances don't carry certain powers—substances do not change the content of your thoughts. Under this umbrella, we show our readers that substances change very little about their thoughts, beliefs, moods, and actions.

There are effects that substances are said to have that are sensational and warrant careful critical thinking. For example, substances are said to have the power to addict people, provide pleasures that outweigh any non-substance activity ("euphoria"), lower inhibitions, cause violence and aggression, or relieve emotional distress. These effects are far harder to pin down pharmacologically, and, in fact, in most cases, no plausible pharmacological explanation whatsoever is available. Therefore, some of these believed effects may not even be a direct or an indirect result of the chemical action of the substance on the body and brain at all. Other effects involve pharmacology, but not in the straightforward way you've been led to believe. A nuanced understanding of this is eye-opening.

Throughout the 20th century, many researchers have uncovered the fact that what people believe about substances, and the circumstances in which they use them, plays a far greater role than pharmacology in what people experience while using substances. To stress the importance of these other factors, some have said that the "drug, set, and setting" should all equally be considered when discussing the effects of intoxication.

1. Drug refers to the actual pharmacological effects of a substance.

2. Set refers to psychological factors, such as the mindset of the individual taking the substances, including beliefs, expectations, intentions, and more.

3. Setting refers to the social, physical, and cultural environment/circumstances in which substances are taken and the information this conveys to the substance user (it is essentially another aspect of mindset).

Sociologists who observe drinking practices have noted that the same amount of the drug alcohol may be taken in a pub or at a wake and seem to have significantly different effects. At the pub, drinkers may become euphoric, talkative, aggressive, and jovial and engage in behaviors considered inappropriate, such as being overly flirtatious, making sexual advances, or speaking in off-color ways. At the wake, drinkers may become dysphoric, quiet, and reserved, talk in hushed and sensitive tones, weep, and become more proper and polite. Let's pick this example apart from the drug, set, and setting point of view.

The actual drug effects of a few drinks of alcohol are: a rise in pulse rate and blood pressure, impaired coordination, and a release of endorphins (which can be perceived as pleasurable). These physical effects brought on by the pharmacological action of the drug will happen equally to the drinker at the pub and the drinker at a wake.

Though it's interesting to note that, even though the endorphin action happens to both, the drinker at the wake may not be feeling pleasure.

The set effects are those that come from the mindset of the individual, including his thoughts, beliefs, and intentions. Most go to the pub with the intention of having a good time, socializing, and presenting a fun-loving image to others. They believe alcohol facilitates these things, so when the physical effects of the alcohol are felt, they begin to feel more sociable, euphoric, and stimulated. Most go to the wake with the intention of mourning the passing of a loved one, showing their pain and sorrow to others who care, and commiserating with them. They believe alcohol facilitates these things, so when they drink, they begin to feel they are more able to express their sadness, to cry, and show their negative emotions as well as concern for others who are also mourning.

The setting effects are those that people are cued to experience by the environment (both physical and social). The pub may feature loud music or noisy sports games on an array of televisions. This tells the patrons it's acceptable to be loud and boisterous. The wake features somber music at a low volume. This tells the mourners they should remain quiet and reserved. The pub is full of people looking to get away from life's responsibilities for a while and have a good time. This tells people it's acceptable to smile, be jovial, and let go of the worries they have outside the pub. The wake is full of people looking to show their respect, offer a shoulder to cry on, or find support from others. This tells people it's a place for quiet and sensitivity. The pub may feature a pool table, darts, or other amusements, or open spaces such as a dance floor. This tells patrons that they can be stimulated and active. The wake may be held in a home, funeral home, or some other type of hall, where the space is filled with tables and seating, active open space is scarce, and there are no forms of entertainment offered. This tells the mourners to be subdued in their behavior. Moreover, the social landscape at the wake is filled with several generations; deference to elders is expected, and care is given to set a good example for the children in attendance. In contrast, the pub may often feature a more limited age group with people closer in age and class as peers, and this has wildly different social dynamics that lead to extremely different behaviors. The presence or absence of relatives in these settings further changes the social expectations and thus the "effects" of drinking in these situations.

These examples of a wake and a pub may resonate with you, or you may be thinking your experience at wakes and pubs is very different. Either way, the point still holds. Wakes can be very different depending on the culture, ethnicity, local customs, or religious orientation of the primary participants involved. The behavior we attribute to alcohol can be extremely different depending on whether it's an Irish pub, a biker bar, a cocktail lounge, a dive bar, a gay bar, an after-hours spot, a sports bar, or a commercial dance club. Each of these settings sends different messages to the drinker, and each is often approached with a different mindset. These variations prove the point that most of the emotional and behavioral effects that get attributed to alcohol have little to do with the direct pharmacology of the drug ethanol. If the pharmacology ruled the behavioral and psychological effects of drugs, then you wouldn't see variation in these effects from place to place, person to person, and even from one day to the next in the same place within the same person. Set and setting wouldn't matter. But they obviously do. You don't need to look through a microscope or at a brain scan to see evidence of this – it is available to the naked eye of anyone who chooses to look.

Because alcohol is used so openly, it lends itself to this analysis easily. Everyone has seen plenty of different outcomes from the use of alcohol. This applies across all intoxicants as well. People approach various drugs with different expectations and intentions, and this plays a massive role in the effects they feel when using. The same applies to settings.

Columbia University neuroscientist and drug researcher, Dr. Carl Hart, PhD, has said that the prescription amphetamines Adderall and Ritalin are nearly identical in chemical composition and effect to the street version of methamphetamine. These different versions of amphetamines work in the brain in slightly different ways, yet all increase cognitive abilities, enhance the ability to concentrate and focus, relieve fatigue, and raise blood pressure and pulse. Moreover, when given in a laboratory to test subjects who are seasoned illegal meth users, they cannot tell the difference between the two (methamphetamine and d-amphetamine [prescription]; Sullum, 2014).

Dr. Hart has been talking publicly about these facts about amphetamines to combat drug hysteria on a societal level. He says that we should see the legal and illegal versions of amphetamines as basically equivalent and notes that we shouldn't fear legal amphetamines more because of this. Until now, the public has been hyped into believing amphetamines are an especially "addictive" drug, yet their legal counterparts (Adderall and Ritalin, among others) are used by people in ways that don't even resemble "addiction." They are often used to good effect, helping some people to have more energy, concentrate better, and become more productive.

There are plenty of methamphetamine users out there who are productive, accomplished people. They use a little bit now and then to give them a boost. There are regular users as well, such as a string of celebrities given meth by a physician the Secret Service dubbed "Dr. Feelgood". His clients included President John F. Kennedy, Nelson Rockefeller, Twilight Zone producer/writer Rod Serling, composer Leonard Bernstein, and playwrights and authors, such as Henry Miller, Anais Nin, and Tennessee Williams. (Getlen, 2013) They are all highly productive legends in their respective fields, seen as making very positive contributions to our culture.

Today, despite the fact that the chemical makeup has not changed, meth is now seen as a drug that turns people into monsters. It's been known to be used by violent biker gang members. Meth users are implicated in all sorts of crimes that are often violent. Dr. Feelgood's amphetamine formula was even taken by the Nazis, and he blames it for turning them into soulless killing machines. Clearly that outcome was a result of the "set and setting" rather than a result of the substance itself.

This "drug, set, and setting" relationship has been well known to researchers and academics for several decades. Unfortunately, it has not been well known to the public nor to the police, anti-drug crusaders, government officials, and the recovery society, all of whom continue to spread overblown myths about the pharmacological effects of substances, both positive and negative.

For an example of a positive myth about the power of a drug, consider the reputation that alcohol has for relieving stress, anxiety, and anger. The recovery society unknowingly promotes this myth with the claim that "alcoholics drink to self-medicate their underlying issues of stress, anxiety, etc.," thereby endowing it with the power to pharmacologically take away negative emotions. They say that anger is a trigger for drinking, purportedly because it has the power to relieve anger or to help people cope with anger. And granted, there is no shortage of people saying things such as "I was so angry that I just needed to have a drink to calm down"

Now, consider the fact that alcohol use is also associated with 40% of violent crimes (Wilcox, 2015). Anger is an emotion essential to the motivation of violence. How is it that alcohol could calm you of your stress and anxiety and take your anger away, yet stimulate and agitate people as well, in some cases to the point of violence? Of course, this is a contradiction, so alcohol couldn't pharmacologically do both these things. Yet it continues to have the reputation of both causing anger and relieving it.

The truth is that alcohol neither relieves nor causes anger. Set and setting are the factors involved that determine the effects. That is, people's thoughts and beliefs about what alcohol does to them and what's warranted in various situations rule their emotions and behaviors while drinking. Pharmacologically, alcohol sedates, slows down neurotransmission, and, in heavier doses, causes disorientation and loss of equilibrium. It may cause you to slur your words, but it doesn't cause you to utter words that challenge someone to a fistfight. It may cause you to lose your balance and be unable to walk a straight line, but it doesn't cause you to walk up to a man and take a swing at him.

Please don't forget this example of the contradictory powers attributed to alcohol; it's particularly important to the lesson of this section. Your loved one is learning in The Freedom Model that he has full freedom of what he does and feels emotionally when using substances. These are the results of what he thinks and believes, not the results of the pharmacological effects of substances.

YOU CAN'T NEED WHAT DOESN'T HELP YOU

Many family members of substance users buy into the idea that their loved one is using substances to "self-medicate". This actually lends credence to the idea that these people actually do need substances. To need is to "require (something) because it is essential or very important". The recovery society and treatment professionals portray substance users as needing the pharmacological effects of substances to relieve emotional distress and inhibitions. Part of how they do this is by putting forward theories that say substance users have either a preexisting chemical imbalance or that substances have changed their brains to the point where the only thing that can make them feel good is more substances. They repeat claims about the emotional powers of substances—that they soothe anger and help with trauma and relieve depression and anxiety and other emotional issues. They push the theory that those who've suffered trauma have had their brains permanently changed in a way that leaves them with levels of stress, which can be "self-medicated" with substances. And finally, they claim that without "alternative coping methods", the "addict" will be forced back to using substances. This all implies that substances can pharmacologically relieve emotional pain and thus can be "needed" for such purposes if nothing else is available.

We are presenting to our readers the view that substances don't serve these purposes and thus can't be "needed" to serve them. Just as you can't need a cupcake to treat a tumor, you can't need alcohol to take away your anxiety. It's possible for someone to believe she needs a cupcake to treat a tumor. Her perception of a need and desperate want of a cupcake wouldn't be any less real because it's motivated by a falsehood, but if she learned that cupcakes don't treat or cure tumors, then she would stop wanting it for that reason. She might still desire a cupcake for the taste and nourishment, but such a level of desire is far lower than what she felt when she believed she "needed" it.

PLACEBO EFFECT AND ACTIVE PLACEBOS

To further illuminate the subject, The Freedom Model discusses the phenomenon of placebo effects. In medical research, placebos have traditionally been pills that have no active ingredients. Some are made of sugar, which is why they're often referred to as "sugar pills". There are also placebo injections (usually saline is used) and placebo procedures where patients were cut and sewn back up, as if they had been given a meaningful medical procedure. (One of these cases was a knee surgery, and those who got the placebo surgery actually had better long-term outcomes than those who got the real surgery). The role of the placebo in research is to find out whether a given treatment is effective or some other forces are at play, causing patients to feel better. Those other forces could be things such as patients' own immune system, perceptions of symptoms, the limited natural course of a disease, or the expectancy of recovery and changes they make to their lifestyles because of expected improvement.

Many prescription drug trials split their test subjects into a group who receives the medication with active ingredients and a group who receives a placebo pill with no active ingredients. Logic holds that if those who receive the real medication experience more improvement in signs and symptoms, then the drug has a positive effect, and if they don't do better than the placebo group, then the drug doesn't work. This practice has taught researchers more than whether prescription drugs work—it has taught them that expectancy is a powerful force. It has taught them that expecting to get well can make people get well for many conditions.

Not surprising, the area where placebos have the biggest effect is in psychiatric medicine. Many antidepressant trials have shown that placebos work almost as well as the real drugs at relieving depression. Interestingly, in both those who receive the real drug and those who receive the placebo, those who experience more side effects are more likely to recover from depression. This encouraged the researchers to try testing the antidepressants against something called an active placebo, which is "a real drug that produces side effects, but that should not have any therapeutic benefits for the condition being treated."

To understand the active placebo, you must first consider what it's like to be involved in a prescription drug trial. You're depressed; you sign up for this new drug trial in the hopes that this will be the miracle drug that finally relieves your condition. You sit down with the doctor to sign consent forms and get a rundown of what to expect. He tells you that you may get an inert placebo or you may get the real drug. He then tells you that you might be getting some bad side effects, such as dry mouth or drowsiness. Then you get your bottle of pills, not knowing whether they're the real thing or not. But if after taking them for a week or two, you don't necessarily feel better yet and you also haven't had any dry mouth or drowsiness, you begin to think you're not on the real drug. Disappointment sets in, and you start to believe you won't get any better because you're on the placebo. This is called "breaking blind" because you were supposed to be blinded to whether you were on the real drug, but you figured it out anyway.

The other side of this is that if you do start to experience dry mouth and drowsiness, you think, 'Yay, I'm on the real drug; I'm gonna get over my depression!' In this case, you've also broken blind. As you can imagine, this causes an obstacle for researchers trying to figure out whether the drugs are truly effective because breaking blind modifies expectations and it becomes impossible to tell whether the patients' depression was relieved by their expectations or by the pharmacological effects of the drug. So, with some of these antidepressants researchers decided to use an active placebo, which is a drug that has none of the active antidepressant ingredients but contains some ingredients that will produce the same side effects, such as dry mouth and drowsiness. This heightened the placebo effect so that, in 78% of antidepressant trials where active placebo was used, there was no clinically significant difference in outcomes between those taking the drug and those taking the placebo (Kirsch, 2010, p. 20).

The lesson here is this: many of the psychological/emotional effects you think you get from drugs aren't directly caused by the pharmacological action of the drug. In this case, the patients developed expectancy that the pill they were taking would improve their mood. They connected it with side effects, fleshing out the expectancy a little more to, "if I get dry mouth and drowsiness, I am on the real drug, it has taken effect, and my mood will improve." Then, when they experience those side effects, they take them as a cue to become optimistic, and this improves their mood.

This active placebo effect has been present in all the examples we reviewed earlier with other substances. You expect alcohol to relieve your anger, you know that when you start to feel tipsy or warm the alcohol is taking effect on your body, and then bingo, you allow yourself to let go of your anger. It is you and your mind relieving your anger, not the alcohol.

Researchers Norman Zinberg (1984) and Andrew Weil (1998) were among the first to run a controlled study on the effects of marijuana in people who had no experience with the drug and had never seen anyone else do it and thus had very few if any expectations of its effects. They did this at Harvard in the late 1960s. Weil came out of it with this conclusion:

"To my mind, the best term for marijuana is active placebo—that is, a substance whose apparent effects on the mind are actually placebo effects in response to minimal physiological action." (p. 96)

He went on to say that "all drugs that seem to give highs" are also active placebos. Note that this isn't a denial that the drugs people take have pharmacological effects that agitate their bodies and brains in some way. But it is a more nuanced understanding of how people seem to get psychological effects from using these drugs. And since the expectancies of what a drug will do vary from person to person, place to place, and time to time, this makes sense of the illogically contradictory effects attributed to drugs. Those effects aren't really coming from the drugs; they're coming from a combination of the drug, set, and setting, and the active placebo model ties it all together.

Throughout Chapter 17 of *The Freedom Model for Addictions* and the subsequent chapters, Chapter 18 "Emotional Relief," Chapter 19 "License to Misbehave," and Chapter 20 "Pleasure," The Freedom Model challenges all of the perceived effects and benefits that people believe they are getting and can get from substances. This information allows readers to make a more accurate assessment of their preference and opens the door to the possibility that they can be happier making an adjustment. Learning that a drug doesn't really take away your anger, depression, or anxiety can make a major dent in your desire for that drug!

CHAPTER 6:

OVERCOMING GUILT, FEAR, AND WORRY

J ust like substance use can become habitual and problematic for the substance user, so too can the emotions of guilt, fear, and worry for those who love them. For parents, spouses, siblings, children, and others close to a heavy substance user, these negative emotions can become all consuming. When talking with families I often hear how they have sought help from mental health professionals and physicians for their own chronic depression, anxiety, and, in some cases, crippling panic attacks.

The intense worry that parents and loved ones feel today, especially parents of those using heroin and other opiates, can be overwhelming. Additionally, many parents and spouses, in particular, may feel intense guilt for not having been "the perfect parent" or "the perfect spouse." They may look at a past divorce, an affair, perceived physical and emotional abuse, or other issues they faced within their own lives that may have affected the substance user as being a cause for the substance user's problems today. It's very important to understand that these feelings are to a great extent within your power to change, and they are, by and large, not accurate and certainly not helpful to anyone.

GUILT—CAN IT BE PRODUCTIVE?

Guilty feelings arise when an individual does something they personally judge is wrong. After experiencing guilt, one might immediately fix the offending behavior and move on. Sometimes guilt is quickly forgotten or ignored, but persists until the behavior is addressed, or we choose to repeat guilt-inducing situations before deciding to change the offending behavior.

Guilt is a natural emotion designed to tell you to stop an offensive choice or behavior. When you listen to your emotions with clarity and maturity, you can decide to stop the behaviors or choices that cause guilty feelings. This is the productive use of guilt: it can motivate positive change in one's life. You can, of course, also choose to avoid remedying the situation and leave it to fester. This decision to avoid responsibility for our behaviors and choices can transform the original emotion of guilt into a deeper, more painful form of long-term shame.

Obviously, productive episodes of guilt exist. But this comes with a very important caveat. Guilt can only be classified as a productive motivator when it is valid and when you are willing to correct the behaviors that cause it. Guilt is an emotion that exists to help you steer your life away from hurtful scenarios and help you move past them. Productive guilt is simply guilt feelings that are valid (because we have done something to create these legitimate feelings), and those feelings can then motivate positive change in ourselves and the world around us.

Sometimes guilt can be based on a fairly important, large-scale mistake we have made, like an affair, embezzling from work, or stealing from our loved ones or neighbors. All of these guilty behaviors can be stopped and rectified through a process of self change and making right a wrong whenever possible.

If your loved one has been in a 12-Step program in the past or has done a treatment program based on it, they may have come to you to make "amends" by saying they're sorry for their behavior. You may be familiar with this and have experienced this kind of self-ingratiating atonement over and over again. The sole purpose of it, as told by the recovery society, is to diminish guilty feelings in the substance users so as not to be "triggered" into using substances again. Unfortunately, most people who engage in this kind of atonement do reoffend, then use their disease as an excuse (you may have heard the common saying in recovery circles, "we practice progress, not perfection"), and their relationships continue to deteriorate. *The Freedom Model for Addictions* takes on this misguided practice head on for the substance user, but what about the guilt felt by those close to the substance user?

Much guilt felt by the heavy substance user is earned and can only be fixed by changing their behaviors. The guilt felt by family members and others close to the substance user is, more times than not, invalid and serves no purpose, as there is nothing you can do to make someone use or not use substances. Certainly that is not to say that you've been perfect within the relationship; no one and no relationships are perfect. Perhaps you and your spouse divorced and it was hard on your children. Maybe you stayed with a spouse who was abusive to you and the children too long. Maybe you had an affair on your spouse or maybe as a child you picked on your sibling mercilessly. Could these transgressions be the cause of your loved one's drug and alcohol problems today?

As was said earlier, people use all sorts of reasons for using substances—but these are reasons for use and not causes of it. Many times substance users will point to something you have done and tell you their behavior is your fault, but even they know that's not the truth. As I talked about previously in the section on enabling, the only behavior for which you're responsible is your own. You can only control yourself. This doesn't give you license to abuse the substance user or mistreat those around you, but it does give you a new perspective on the guilt you may be feeling for things you may have done in the past. This information should help you to understand that you no longer have to feel guilt or the need to rehash old hurts and past transgressions with the substance user. You can let go of any on-going conflict about what you did 1, 5, or 20 years ago, and stop blaming yourself for this person's behaviors today. You can also choose not to participate in the blame game by refusing to take on the substance user's misplaced accusations, anger, and blame.

Whether or not people bring past problems into their present is a choice and using past mistakes or transgressions of others to excuse or explain away their chosen behaviors today is a recipe for a troubled life. This is covered explicitly for substance users in The Freedom Model, where they learn that the only thing that determines whether they'll use substances or not today is their own view of whether they believe they need it for happiness today or not.

Some people wear their guilt like a badge of honor. They feel guilty for their successes and their failures. They compare themselves to others and may feel jealousy for those who have more than them, and then they may feel guilt because they have more than someone else. This habitual guilt can have a negative effect on your relationships and your life overall. If this behavior is overly problematic for you, then perhaps it would be wise to seek out a solution-based therapist for help.

It's important to understand if you have been successful in life, you've earned that success. As they say, good luck is the residue of preparation. You needn't and shouldn't feel guilty that you don't have the struggles of someone else. Each person's success and failure are solely their responsibility alone.

Letting misplaced guilt direct your relationship with a substance user is ill-advised and can cause significant problems for you and for the substance user. Learning to differentiate productive guilt, which can guide a change in your behavior for the better, from unfounded and misplaced guilt, is crucial to being able to shed that unproductive guilt from your life. When you do, you will open the door to changing your relationship with the substance user and also gaining self-confidence and a higher level of satisfaction in your own life.

OVERCOMING FEAR AND WORRY HABITS

The underlying cause of many negative emotions and behaviors is fear. Fears reinforce negative thinking and eventually can diminish positive thoughts and emotions. Some substance users who live in a constant state of fear of responsibility are frightened by the work needed to grow and develop past their problems. With fear as their primary motivator, as is the case in treatment, positive life changes are slowed dramatically or may come to a complete stop.

In the case of family members and friends of substance users, their lives can become consumed with fear and worry that the substance user will get hurt, sick, or die. You may have spent many sleepless nights waiting for the substance user to get home safely or long days waiting for a returned call or text. Perhaps the substance user has already survived a severe accident or overdose, so your anxiety is now heightened. You can't watch the local news without learning of some tragedy attributed to drug use or drinking, and each time you think, that could be my son, daughter, sibling, spouse, friend, or parent. There is no doubt that fear and worry for your loved one's safety can take a toll on your life and health.

How can you alleviate the fear, worry, and stress caused by the behaviors of those you love? It is important to understand the reason for your anxiety. It is caused by legitimate feelings of powerlessness and helplessness. You should know by now beyond a doubt that you cannot control the behaviors of others, no matter how much you want to control them. The only answer then is to take the necessary actions to gain control of the only life you can control: your own. Make plans for your future that don't include contingencies for the substance user's behaviors. Assume they will continue on their current path, while hoping they will change, but make plans for your own happiness and fulfillment regardless of their choices. You have learned through this book that you can shed all misplaced guilt, and now it is time for you to make plans to enjoy your life and successes.

If the substance user is still in your life, especially if they are living with you, it is ok to set higher expectations for him and be clear about what those expectations are up front. If you don't want illicit drugs in your home, let him know this and be firm. You can be assertive without being angry, offensive, or threatening. If you do not want to be around your loved one when she is drinking or intoxicated, say so calmly but firmly. Let her know you are moving on with your life, regardless of her behaviors, and be clear about what, if any, help you are willing to provide in the future.

You can explain to the substance user that you have learned you can't control his behaviors and nor should you, as he is entitled to live his life the way he sees fit, so now it is time for you to build a happier life for yourself. It is important to keep in mind the substance user is making choices for his life, too; he is not suffering from a disease, and he is definitely not powerless. Some of the consequences of the substance user's choices and behaviors may be sickness or unemployment, family or legal troubles, or even death, but he is aware of these potential consequences, and if he continues heavy use, know that he is willing to accept them. Ultimately, his choices truly have nothing to do with you and that knowledge can and should be freeing for you.

Of course, be prepared for your resolve to be tested. You will have to decide if you will follow through on your plans and what you are willing to do for the substance user. When that time comes, whatever you decide to do should not be done out of fear or guilt, as these are needless emotions that get in the way of you achieving your goals. What you decide to do should be based on what will make you happier at that moment and what is in line with your goals. Keep in mind, too, what you choose to do will have little or no bearing whatsoever on future decisions your loved one will make with respect to his substance use. You may provide the help he's seeking from you, and he may run right back to the situation that landed him in trouble in the first place; or he may finally decide his life is unacceptable to him and make a change. But he is equally likely to do either of these whether you provide him help or let him work out his problems on his own.

Some people find peace through a spiritual life or through their chosen faith or religion. Be aware some religions encourage moral judgment and guilt, which may compound your fears, resentments, and other negative emotions, but practicing a faith on a personal level can also help ease fear and worry. This depends on your perspective and goals. Many people include some form of spiritual goals when working to create a more fulfilling and happy future.

Additionally, there are many natural remedies and activities that can lessen anxiety, such as walking, yoga, light stretching, golfing, swimming, horseback riding, boating, fishing, meditation, or spending time with close family or friends. The key is to find activities you enjoy and set up a schedule to do them regularly. As we get older, and especially when we spend much of our time caring for others, we tend to forget to have fun and take time out to do things we enjoy. We must re-learn to play, and then make it a priority within our busy schedules.

Some people seek the help of a therapist, but once again, caution is recommended. A good therapist will not simply listen to your problems, suggest you go to a meeting, or write you a prescription. An effective therapist will help you put things in perspective and give you concrete ways to adjust your thinking, focusing on things you can change about yourself only. There is no point spending hours in therapy talking about how you wish others would behave differently, because you have no power to change them. A good therapist will instead steer the conversation to areas of your life that you can change.

When seeking a therapist, it is important to find someone who is focused on solutions, and not on rehashing the past over and over again. A great place to find a therapist is at www.psychologytoday. com where you can enter your location and find a detailed listing of therapists in your immediate area. When you click on a profile there is a category called Treatment Orientation. You want to look for professionals who utilize some of the most effective therapy methods such as Cognitive Behavorial Therapy (CBT), Mindfulness Based (MBCT), Motivational Interviewing, and Solution-Focused therapies. You may want to avoid those who specialize in treating addiction and helping families with addiction issues, as they are likely rooted in the disease paradigm, and will recommend you attend support meetings such as Al-Anon and other 12 Step groups which are ineffective and, in some cases, harmful.

Whether or not you choose to seek therapy is a very personal decision and is not for everyone. Furthermore you may not feel you need it, once you gain a new perspective on addiction. Many people become overly anxious or fearful because they are focused on the worst-case scenario. They engage in exaggerated negative self-talk and their fears become over-inflated. Like substance users who learn that cravings are simply repetitive thoughts over which they do have control, you also have control over your thoughts of dread and doom.

To address these thoughts, it's important to put your worries and fears into perspective. Millions of people use drugs and alcohol every day and only a tiny percentage of those who use heavily and daily die suddenly as a direct result of their substance use. Yes, rates of overdose are increasing at a high rate (which is largely due to the deadly combination of addiction disease ideology and prohibition which created black market drugs), but the numbers are still very, very low. Turn off the news and stay off social media if it is increasing your anxiety. And remember that people are in far more danger riding in a car or being treated in a hospital for any reason than they are smoking a joint, having a drink, or taking a dose of heroin, cocaine, or other drugs.

Each time you begin to feel panic or your fear and worry get in the way of your happiness, quickly replace that thought with something that brings you joy and relaxation, perhaps a goal you are working on or upcoming plans with friends. Your worry serves no purpose and can only hurt you. As you consciously, systematically, identify those thoughts and feelings and replace them, you will notice your negative thoughts becoming less frequent. They will never go away entirely, but they will become manageable and based more on reality and not on your worst fears of what might happen. This is called faithful thinking. It has nothing to do with religion or spirituality but rather faith that things will be ok, because they nearly always are. Faithful thinking requires practice and diligence, but you will see you do have control over your worst case scenario thoughts.

Remember, most substance users do change their lives at some point. As long as they know they have the ability to change, the likelihood is great they will change eventually. Unfortunately, traditional treatment and our disease-based culture have perpetuated the myth, "once an addict, always an addict," which is not only untrue, but damaging as well. For many family members of substance users, this erroneous belief has caused endless worry, doubt, and fears. Now that the myths have been dispelled, you are truly free to get on with your life knowing full well your loved one is able to change his/her life.

Sadly, there are times when things don't work out, when a worst case scenario happens; what purpose did ongoing worry serve? In retrospect you can see that it didn't serve any purpose as the outcome happened regardless. In some cases, our constant focus on a worst case scenario, and acting on our fears can actually bring about a negative outcome. The law of attraction states that which we focus on, can become our reality. Focus on the positive usually begets positive outcomes while focusing on the negative can literally bring about negative outcomes. By breaking the worry habit, and expecting positive outcomes, you will see more positive happen in your life. Additionally, you will become more able to emotionally handle tragedies and trauma as they happen because they happen for everyone.

As we said at the beginning of this book, the only life you can change is your own. Isn't it time to build the life you truly want? Don't you deserve happiness and success and to enjoy the fruits of your labors? Of course you do, everyone does. Guilt, shame, worry, anxiety, you do have control over these emotions, and you have lived with them long enough. Make a plan to minimize these thoughts from your everyday life, and build the life you want your loved one to emulate. Just as you have no control over her behavior, show her that she no longer has any control over your life. Plan for a happy future and feel great about it. It's infectious and you have no idea the profound effects it will have on those around you.

If it is helpful to you, put your plans for your future in writing and begin discussing them with your friends and family today. It is likely they have been waiting for this and will be excited to help you move forward in your life.

CHAPTER 7:

WHAT ABOUT AFTERCARE? DO PEOPLE NEED SUPPORT?

The addiction recovery culture aggressively promotes the idea that substance users require extensive aftercare and support to remain sober and drug free. As a result many family members and friends expect that their loved one will need to go to meetings, therapy and have ongoing counseling to stay the course and maintain "recovery" once he/she completes *The Freedom Model for Addictions*. This faulty belief is a direct result of the popularity of the 12-step program, Alcoholics Anonymous. If you ask someone on the street what they think is the most effective way for problem drinkers to stop drinking, most everyone will say, "Go to AA." Yet, research data consistently shows the most effective way for people to stop an addiction is to do it on their own. (For supporting research and documentation read Chapter 1 of *The Freedom Model for Addictions*.)

Throughout this book you have learned the importance of beliefs with respect to expectations and behaviors. 12-step programs such as Alcoholics Anonymous and Narcotics Anonymous foster a belief system rooted in powerlessness. People are taught they must rely on external factors like God, meetings and sponsors for continued sobriety. But what happens when a sponsor leaves the program and uses alcohol or drugs as so many do? What about when a substance user's faith in God or a Higher Power is tested as it is for all people of Faith at some point in life? What about those with no belief in a higher being or those who are more private and less social? For AA members, relapse is an expected part of lifelong recovery, and while they see it as a symptom of the disease, AA members often cast harsh judgments and treat those who "slip" and drink or use drugs badly when they return to meetings.

As you have read The Freedom Model offers a completely different understanding of addiction and substance use problems. Our readers have learned they have complete control over their thoughts, behaviors, actions and reactions, and they learned the immense benefits of being proactive in all areas of life. They have identified the reasons why they prefer substances and intoxication and they have explored the possibility that they can be happier by adjusting their substance use.

Chapter 13 of *The Freedom Model for Addictions* is focused on success. It talks about how people change a substance use habit or any other habit and paints the supposed need for aftercare in a different light. It asks the following: "How do you quit a job?" Nobody asks such a question because the answer is incredibly simple. You tell your boss "I quit," and then you don't return there to work. The real issue is whether you want to quit that job or keep working there. Do you see a better alternative? Do you think it's worth leaving that job? Do you think you'll be happier if you do? The answers to such questions determine whether you'll want to quit, and then the actual nuts and bolts of quitting are simple; you just say "I quit" and then go on your merry way. You don't need to resist going back to that job every day and you certainly don't need support for it.

"How do I quit drinking/drugging?" is the same sort of question. It is fully a matter of figuring out what you want. When you know what that is, you just do it. It doesn't take any strength or willpower or support to not do what you know you don't want to do. It doesn't take any special techniques or steps. There's no effort needed to maintain not drinking or drugging (or moderating those activities), just as there is no effort needed to not work at the job you quit. The effort is simply in figuring out what you really want and then naturally moving in that new direction.

Unfortunately, people don't realize how simple this truly is because recovery ideology and its proponents have confused the issue so much with their misinformation. They've led people into believing they're not free to make their own choices about substance use. They make you think it's highly complicated, that it's an ongoing process, that some sort of treatment or support is needed, and that it requires a lifelong struggle. In short, they've taught your loved one that he is not free to change by the normal powers of choice that he applies to other problems. Such beliefs are all that stand in the way of anyone making a change in his or her level of substance use.

It is those faulty beliefs that lead to increased rates of heavy continuous use and dangerous binge use among people that attend 12 step meetings and treatment based on it. It is estimated that at the end of one month 50% of AA attendees have stopped going to meetings, and 95% have stopped by the end of one year. This is a testament to the reality that no amount of support or external factors can stop people from doing what they really want to do and what they believe will make them happy.

Our society doesn't seem to have the patience or tolerance to let people be, to let them make these decisions for themselves. It often tries to coerce people into changing their substance use habits. The legal system is used for this purpose by threatening jail time and other sanctions. Families try to do this by means of "tough love." The treatment system tries to coerce substance users into agreeing to abstinence by equating heavy substance use with a disease, so that they will blindly obey the doctors' orders. And, from every corner, shame is heaped on substance users. They are told that their preferred mode of substance use is dysfunctional, disordered, diseased, and bad. Their substance use is negatively judged, and they are socially sanctioned for it in any number of ways.

Then, they are assigned the goal of abstinence from all substance use and adoption of the recovery lifestyle. With this goal, comes a standard of "success"; if you don't adopt and fulfill complete abstinence and "recovery" as your goal, you are declared a failure. If you choose moderation, you are a failure. Even if you abstain fully or moderate to socially acceptable levels but do so without also adopting the recovery lifestyle which includes ongoing meetings and therapy, you're considered a failure. This is a no-win situation where success becomes nothing more than compliance with the demands of others. To the substance user caught in this coercive game, the idea of success loses its positive personal meaning.

Put all this coercion and the addiction myths together, and you end up with a whole lot of people who do not feel free to make their own choices about substance use. Many try to quit out of shame and coercion and then wonder why they "relapsed." From the Freedom Model perspective, the "relapse" is just a choice to do what you believe will make you happy. Their quit attempt came from fear and coercion; it didn't come from a sense of freely pursuing the happiest option. They felt cornered into quitting, but they didn't really see moderation or abstinence as happier, more fulfilling options. This is the source of most reversed attempts to quit or adjust substance use: people don't feel free to make their own choices. They make these failed attempts based on doing what others think they should do or what they've been scared into doing, not on what they wholeheartedly believe will make them happiest.

The results are that, while abstaining, they are unhappy, and when returning to substance use, they are also unhappy, but with a little bit of pleasure on top of the misery. This becomes a vicious cycle that can chew up people's lives for decades and spit them out feeling doomed to perpetual failure.

This cycle leaves families angry, frustrated and devoid of hope. We, the Freedom Model authors, were stuck in this cycle too and didn't get out of it until we realized we were free to do so. We have now helped thousands of people take themselves out of this cycle over the years by showing them that they are free too. Thus, here is our definition of success in The Freedom Model: success is knowing that you are free and happily choosing what you see as best for you.

In The Freedom Model, our goal is to show substance users they are completely free to choose to change their use of substances in whatever way they see fit. If they feel this freedom after considering the ideas and information we've presented, then that is a successful outcome regardless of what choices they make regarding substance use.

We want our readers to gain complete and total independence and autonomy, to learn they can solve their problems through learning the facts about substance use and addiction and then make an informed decision of how they wish to proceed to achieve greater personal happiness. Over three decades, an average of 62% of our retreat graduates have achieved long-term abstinence based on independent surveys (Baldwin Research). While that is truly outstanding, it also means 38% of program graduates chose to continue substance use in some fashion. Some (perhaps more than half) of the substance-using group successfully moderate their behaviors and report success in many areas of life. This finding is consistent with independent research that shows that most problems drinkers and even those once classified as alcoholic, moderate their alcohol use rather than abstain completely. (Sobbell, et.al.) Some in the using group report choosing to continue what their families consider problematic and/or excessive use, but many of them admit knowing they are in control and can make the choice to stop or moderate at any time.

There are those in the using group who stay devoted to a victim and disease mentality. But in the end, this too, is a choice. Most of our guests at our retreats have been exposed to 12-step programs, have had two or more stints in rehab and have had addiction counseling and therapy. Although they do have control, for some, sticking with their old beliefs allows them to continue their chosen lifestyle with little or no personal accountability and responsibility. This is important for families to know and consider when dealing with someone who returns to heavy substance use and the problems that often go with it. In these cases the substance user sees benefits in maintaining the addict/alcoholic identity. It is then up to families to decide whether or not they will continue to participate in the charade.

It is important to note that some who complete *The Freedom Model for Addictions* at our retreats do return to what families consider excessive or problematic use for a period of days, weeks, or months, resulting in more trouble. Then, seemingly overnight, they stop. They decide they can be happier by changing their substance use, do just that and move on with their lives. As the SAMHSA statistics and various other independent research shows, most people stop substance use problems at some point in their lives and have a much greater chance of doing so once they know they can.

In cases where the individual returns home and continues heavy substance use, it is up to you, the family, friends and relatives to decide how much more of this behavior you are willing to tolerate, how you want to proceed and what additional help, if any, you are willing to provide. Thankfully, you can do this with a clear conscience, knowing the substance user is not suffering from a disease and is, instead, choosing a lifestyle, fully knowing it is a choice. You need not provide care and resources any longer at the expense of your own happiness, finances and peace of mind. You can finally move on with your life comfortable with your decision, knowing the only life you can control is your own.

THE PROBLEM WITH REPLACEMENT

Many family members believe that substance users must use replacement therapy drugs and/or find alternate activities to keep them sober and drug free. This belief system is the result of the deep-rooted addiction and recovery culture in this country. As such many people try to find alternative activities to pit against substance use, things to take up their time and distract them from their desire for substance use. They often think they must come up with something spectacular to replace heavy substance use. While these strategies seem intuitively correct, they unnecessarily complicate the process of change and distract people from the real issue, which is centered in substances and their preferences for them.

One popular replacement activity is going to the gym. Many people get some mileage out of this, and it seems to work. But what happens when they get sick, are too tired, or just don't have time for the gym? They are left without an activity to deal with the abstinence that they have been forced to choose but don't prefer. Eventually, if they never preferred abstinence as being more attractive than heavy substance use, then they will feel what the recovery culture calls a "craving." They may wonder, 'Why am I having a craving now I have been replacing alcohol with the gym for several weeks? Shouldn't I be over the hump? Shouldn't the fact that I am working out produce the energy and good feelings needed to replace the desire for substances?' The truth is, the hump has very little to do with reality; it's just an arbitrary milestone that he set that is a distraction from the reality that he still prefers substances. When the individual finds that the gym, the new workout regimen, or his new focus on nutrition isn't cutting it and he finds he still prefers using substances over those distractions, he inevitably returns to doing what he wants to do: use substances.

That is when he must shift his thinking to those three options:

1. Heavy substance use
2. Adjusted substance use (what most call "moderation")
3. Abstinence

If this individual does not take the time to truly reconsider those options, his preference will likely remain the same, and his desire will nag at him. Of course, it is possible that, in those few weeks of going to the gym, he could also be rethinking these options and discovering he no longer prefers heavy substance use. That is why it is so importantto begin rethinking those options immediately instead of counting on luck and hoping the preference changes by chance.

Life isn't a set of binary choices between going to the gym and getting drunk. So it doesn't make sense to replace drinking with such an activity. Think about it: what happens when he goes to a party? Should he start doing push-ups the moment he thinks of having a drink? What makes more sense is for him to find out if he can be happier without alcohol or with less of it so he can exist happily in any situation, not just in a replacement activity.

Here's another issue to consider with such replacements: while the substance user is refusing to generate a benefits list for the moderation and abstinence options, she is also leaving her opinion of the benefits of heavy substance use fully intact. What she might discover if she critically examines her preference for heavy substance use is that it no longer is as beneficial as it once was to her. That is why *The Freedom Model for Addictions* devotes a quarter of the text to discussing perceived benefits and effects of substances.

With courage, critical thinking, and experiential learning through proactively testing their options, many who have completed *The Freedom Model for Addictions* discover that heavy substance use is boring, unsatisfying and that they do not need it for any sort of relief. Many discover more relief, more excitement, and more happiness in the moderation or abstinence options. But when people jump right into replacement, they are sidestepping these issues. That is like the motorcyclist telling himself he needs to go to the gym to forget his dissatisfaction with the motorcycle he once enjoyed so much. That would be weird, right? That's because it ignores the issue completely, that being his issue with his current ride. In the same respect, preference change doesn't usually happen by replacing it with random and unrelated distractions. Instead people can proactively do something to address their preference for heavy substance use by looking at moderation and abstinence options directly.

The same goes for replacing heavy substance use with "alternative coping methods." These replacements keep people from addressing the preference directly and add another issue to the mix, further complicating it. If your loved one believes that his heavy substance use is a "coping method," that is, as a solution to his problems, he would be better off examining the benefits of it and finding out whether it truly solves any of those problems. Critical thinking shows that it doesn't solve problems, and if he discovered and became convinced of this, he would never feel the desire to use it as a "coping method" again. However, by sidestepping this issue and thinking he needs an alternative coping method, this keeps the idea that substances are a viable "coping method" alive in his mind. Treatment that teaches "alternative coping methods" gives substances credit they don't deserve by putting the use of substances on an almost equal plane with effective coping methods.

Again, what happens when your loved one doesn't want to use those "alternative coping methods" or when they don't seem to work? They are going to experience problems in life that will leave them with frustration and emotional pain. In these cases, they will likely find themselves itching to use substances heavily again as a coping method. Yet, if they address their preference head on and explore the benefits of the three options, they learn that even with various life problems going on, they get more happiness from moderation or abstinence and that heavy use does not help. That change in perception does away with heavy substance use as a potential coping method for good and improves their overall level of happiness.

The primary treatment method for opiate and alcohol use is quickly becoming replacement therapy medications such as naltrexone, methadone and suboxone (buprenorphine). More and more drugs like these will be coming onto the scene over the next few years. The addiction disease paradigm is big business in this country, and people are always seeking that quick fix. Once again while these medications may be helpful during detox, as a long term solution, just like replacement activities and alternative coping methods, they also fail to address the substance user's preference for intoxication. While they are advertised as being able to take away cravings, the fact is pharmacologically no drug has the power to change your thoughts, and a craving is simply a thought that getting high would be great at that moment.

Methadone and suboxone can effectively reduce or eliminate opiate withdrawal symptoms, but they can't change your mind. If your loved one still believes that she can be happier shooting or snorting heroin, and that belief stays intact, she will likely go back to using heroin even after her withdrawal is done and her symptoms are completely abated.

The gym is great. Effective coping methods are great. Even medications can serve a limited purpose. We want our readers to have various goals, aspirations, good health, productive relationships, and all the other joys of life. We encourage them to do everything that they want to do and pursue their own vision of happiness. But to address the issue of a strong preference for heavy substance use head on, the most direct way is to critically and directly explore the benefits of the three options, not replace their current use with unrelated temporary distractions. Heavy substance use problems are seldom so narrowly limited to an extra hour of the day that can be replaced with a trip to the gym or rare moments of stress that simply require a coping method. The preference is usually wider ranging than that. Reassessing the three options allows substance users to address the full depth of the preference. What's more, when they have eliminated their preference for a troubling degree of substance use, they become much more effective at chasing and achieving all those other life improvements they want.

CHAPTER 8:

YOUR LOVED ONE HAS COMPLETED THE FREEDOM MODEL FOR ADDICTIONS

For many parents, relatives and friends, there is much fear and uncertainty as their loved one returns home from one of our retreats. They may be unsure how to act or what to say. If their loved one has been to other programs and failed, the return home starts a waiting game of wondering, did this program work? As I stated previously, there is no program that can make someone choose to stop drinking/drug using and stay stopped. There is no magic pill or medication, no meeting, no sponsor, no support group, no counselor, no rehab, no therapist or doctor that can change what's in a person's heart and mind. The only person who can effect this change or make the choice to not drink/drug is the substance user.

Unlike drug treatment programs your loved one may have attended in the past that teach the substance user they are forever powerless and diseased, The Freedom Model has dispelled those myths, provided the substance user with crucial information, and helped them to address their preference for substance use directly. Once they have completed the course, they know beyond the shadow of a doubt that they are in control of their thoughts and behaviors and always have been. Your loved one gained immense insight into his/her habits, thoughts, motives and behaviors. He identified areas he wanted to change and he has likely made changes already. For some, change is dramatic, rapid and permanent; like a line in the sand demarcating their old life from their new one. For others, it's a learning process that lasts for several weeks or months after they leave the retreat.

For each person it is different, and while most do make significant lifestyle changes, there are some who decide they will not change at all. They decide that they are happy with their life as it is and make the choice to continue a lifestyle and behaviors you had hoped they would not. If they are being honest with themselves and you, even these people will admit they are making a choice. This does not mean they will not change at some point in the future, it simply means that for now, this is the life they want. Throughout The Freedom Model readers are encouraged to be honest with those around them about their intentions, so you, their family and friends, can then make an informed decision for your life. There is good news: based on the data, most people (well over 90%) do eventually stop their addictions. The fact that your loved one has completed *The Freedom Model for Addictions* means they know they can change when they decide that is what they want to do.

ENCOURAGING INDEPENDENCE AND AUTONOMY

Our Freedom Model readers, private instruction students and retreat guests range in age from mid-teens to late 70s, but there is one age group that is most heavily represented and that is young adult: 18-35 years old. The adolescent years (12-20) are a time of intense growth in all areas, physically, emotionally and mentally. It is during this time that children must make the transition from being completely dependent on someone else (usually parents) to becoming independent, mature and autonomous. This transition can be slowed significantly when an individual has severe problems with substance use.

Parents and loved ones who make excuses, mitigate consequences or micromanage their adolescent and adult children, spouse, family member or friend show a complete lack of confidence in them and their abilities. After years of watching the substance user struggle, their expectations of the substance user's capabilities may be extremely low. Sometimes well-meaning family members will manage their adult children's lives, financially, emotionally and otherwise. They may take on raising grandchildren, paying bills, working to get them a job, and setting up appointments, etc. Some provide an apartment, housekeeping and laundry services, transportation, and even set goals for their loved one. As I said previously in the section on enabling, none of these are inherently bad, but there may be unintended negative consequences for both parties involved. It's important to consider this: when you micromanage someone you are giving them a vote of no confidence. You are showing them through your actions that you think they can't; you believe they are powerless, and therefore you must do for them what you believe they can't do for themselves.

As you are beginning to think of your future, it may be time to assess all that you are doing for your loved one and really open your mind to the reality that there is so much he/she can and should be doing for him/herself. And while I am definitely not advocating tough love or cutting the person off, having an open and honest discussion about how this person can become independent and autonomous is warranted and advised. As a parent it's so easy to find yourself in a rut of care-taking for an adult child that is long past the point of needing that kind of care. The same can happen with siblings, spouses and close friends who take on caretaking responsibilities for a heavy substance user, as you may have bought into the idea that your loved one was sick (suffering from the disease of addiction). Now that you know they are not, you can choose to allow them to manage their own responsibilities.

Families may be concerned the substance user has mental illness or severe emotional problems that require more care. As The Freedom Model is not medical, but rather educational, our recommendation with respect to mental health concerns you may have about your loved one is that you seek the advice of a licensed medical or mental health professional. It is important to remember that if your child or loved one is an adult, he/she cannot be forced to see a mental health professional. But if he/she would like to see a mental health professional, I advise caution as not all therapy and counseling have positive outcomes. It is important to shop around and seek a mental health professional who specializes in Cognitive Behavioral Therapy, is not quick to diagnose and medicate, and focuses on empowering clients to solve their problems and move on in their lives. A good therapist who truly wants to help will take the time to learn about *The Freedom Model for Addictions*, and whenever requested we will happily send a complimentary copy to a therapist for you and your loved one. We recommend you put the therapist in contact with our Guest Services staff if they have questions or would like a copy of the book.

Rebuilding and/or repairing strained relationships can be challenging as you each may have developed counterproductive habits. Once your loved one has completed the course, there is no more need for arguing, yelling, or overly dramatic scenes about substance use as depicted on television. It is recommended that you sit down with your loved one and let him/her know what you want for your future. Talk about your plans and how your loved one may fit into those plans if they so choose.

If your loved one is coming back to live with you, even temporarily, it is important for you to communicate the conditions under which she may return and stay so she can then make an informed decision if this is right for her. To make this conversation most productive, I recommend that you set your personal judgments aside and ask your loved one about his/her plans and goals specifically with respect to substance use. Whether you agree with them or not, keep in mind your loved one is an adult and will choose to live however he/she wants to live.

Whatever choice he makes, however he behaves once he's completed the Freedom Model course, allow for the possibility that he is living the life he wants and make your decisions for your life accordingly. Do not allow yourself to be lured into any continued chaos by guilt or fear or in an effort to manipulate or control the substance user. Instead do as much or as little for him as you want to do; and base your decision on what makes you happy and what allows you to sleep at night. Once you actively focus on living your life and allow your loved one to take responsibility for his, you will provide him with an opportunity to examine if he can be happier by making a change.

HOW TO BE SUPPORTIVE WITH THE FREEDOM MODEL

We go to great lengths to show our readers and students that they are in full control of their substance use, that no one is responsible for their substance use other than themselves, and that the onus to change is on them. This means no more excuses, no more triggers, no more "succumbing" to cravings or negative feelings and being forced to "relapse." Most importantly for you, the reader of this book, no more blaming of family, friends, and other loved ones who have only ever tried to help.

It is important to understand that all relationships are a two way street where two parties inhabit particular social roles in how they interact with each other. For example, in a doctor/patient relationship, the doctor needs to be authoritative, confident, and have an answer for the patient, who is sick and unable to solve his problem on his own. Because of this expert/layperson role the patient is usually willing to obediently follow his doctor's orders. If either party fails to fulfill their role, such as the doctor not providing answers, or the patient failing to follow the doctor's orders, the relationship doesn't proceed in the productive way we've come to expect. There are all sorts of formal social roles like this: teacher/student; mother/son; husband/wife; manager/employee; friend/friend; big sister/little sister; priest/parishioner; probation officer/probationer; etc – where people live up to and play out certain expectations.

It takes both parties actively participating to sustain many of these roles, and some relationships may dissolve completely if one party doesn't play along. For example, Freedom Model co-author Steven Slate once had a probation officer who told him "I don't care about you because I have teen moms who sell drugs to worry about. Just don't get arrested again." The PO never called Steven for check-ins on his employment status, or scheduled any kind of regular meetings, and he never even gave Steven a drug test throughout an entire year of probation. During that year Steven continued to use drugs, didn't get steady employment, and continued on his path – in short, Steven didn't act like a man on probation at least in part because his probation officer didn't act like a probation officer. It was as if the relationship didn't exist at all.

There are also less formal social roles that we don't even realize we're playing, and that pigeonhole us and change our expectations of each other. Nerd/cool kid is a good example of this. What is a nerd before he gets treated as such? He's probably just a precocious child who likes learning, and has unique yet unpopular interests. But then he goes to school where conformity and popularity rule the roost.

The other children find his quirks and way of being to be uncool, weird, etc. He may be rejected and picked on for his differences; told that he's unworthy of belonging and sent the message that he's not worthy of having friends and being liked. A separation is made, with some of the children being the cool kids, and him being the nerd. He may then have anxiety about fitting in, which makes him more socially awkward, and make his attempts to fit in and make friends seem more desperate, which makes him seem even less cooler, and it all cascades from there to him being in the role of outcast nerd, and the others being popular and cool. In fact, these two social roles can't exist without each other.

The social roles with which we are most concerned is helpless addict/normal person and in order to be supportive, you must gain a completely different understanding of this relationship and these roles. As "addicts" are just people with a strong preference for substance use, they are not actually helpless or enslaved to substance use. But when people without a strong preference for substance use define themselves as "in control" and define those with a strong preference for substance use as "out of control addicts," it creates the social role of the addict. And these social roles then come with a set of expectations.

The "out of control addict" is seen as fragile and able to be triggered into involuntary substance use. This means his loved ones must be cautious to not upset him, and must actively work to protect him from other potential triggers. Playing his role, the addict can now be "triggered" by loved ones that don't treat him exactly as he wants. He becomes fragile, and as a result can always find a justification to use substances and claim that he couldn't help himself because he was triggered by a fight with dad or his wife; or triggered by someone who drank alcohol in his vicinity, thereby "tempting" him.

The addict is seen as needing to be completely stable emotionally, and protected from any failures or disappointments that may cause a "slip" or "relapse." If those close to him say things like "I'm worried you might relapse, you've been depressed," or after losing a job or romantic relationship they say "this is a tough time, you better get some support so you don't relapse," they are helping to sustain this fragile addict role by treating these imagined weaknesses as real.

All of these "weaknesses" become real to him, because others treat them as real. But what if nobody played along? What if there were no "normal people who can control themselves" to his "helpless addict" role? What if he were treated as fully capable? The "unlikeable nerd" would just be a precocious child with unique interests if he wasn't treated as a nerd. And the "helpless fragile addict" would just become a person who has had a strong preference for heavy substance use who is making his own decisions about substance use, if he were treated that way.

The helpless fragile addict is no more of a reality than Superman. If your child told you he was Superman, would you encourage him to attempt to lift boulders? Would you spend time looking for kryptonite to protect him? Would you walk him up to the roof and tell him to fly? If you did these things, you'd be helping him to sustain an illusion, possibly to disastrous consequences.

So here is the best way you can support your loved one with a substance use problem: treat her as a fully capable person. Stop treating her as a helpless fragile addict who isn't in control of her substance use. She is in control. She is capable of moderation if that is what she wants. She is not caused to "relapse" by emotional problems or any of the other normal difficulties of life. And if the people closest to her stop playing along with this role of the mythological addict, she'll have a much harder time continuing to play that role. If you treat her as capable, she'll have an easier time of returning to the role of a capable person.

This is what the Presenters at our retreats and in our private instruction courses do. They interact with and treat their students as fully in control of their substance use, and fully capable of changing their preference for substance use. They provide the information necessary for our students to understand all of this, and to leave the role of the helpless fragile addict behind them forever.

If someone attending our classes comes to the office lamenting that they've used substances in a way that they regret, and claiming to be weak and helpless, we do not entertain this way of seeing their choice to use substances. We simply ask them what they liked and disliked about their choice, and what choices they think might make them happier. We facilitate a conversation that puts them in the role of being fully free to choose differently and fully capable of changing their preferences. We don't shame them for their substance use; we don't harp on the dangers (although we do make sure all of our students are aware of the genuine dangers). We don't tell them they need more support, or that they must avoid triggers.

We don't go looking for mysterious causes of their substance use. We keep it much simpler and more straight forward than that. We ask them what they think could make them happier and help them to achieve their personal goals. We don't call their usage a relapse or slip, because it isn't either of those things – it is a choice to do a thing that they thought would make them happy, and nothing more. And like any other activity in life, it can be abandoned when the individual believes they'd be happier abandoning it.

We don't expect you to act like one of our Presenters. Our Presenters do not direct our students on what their substance use outcome should be, nor do they have any real stake in the outcome as you have. Their policy is to help the student become informed so that he can discover and feel free to carry out whatever he deems to be his best option for happiness, whether that includes substance use or not. For family members and those close to our students, it's much harder and maybe perhaps inappropriate for you to be disinterested in your loved one's substance use choices. It's important for you to realize though, that you don't have to be happy with your loved one's substance use choices. You can be saddened, disappointed or angry when they use in a way you think is bad or harmful. You can be happy, proud, and elated when they reduce or quit their substance use. That is all quite natural and expected. Nevertheless, you can have whatever reaction is natural to you, while still refusing to treat them as a helpless, fragile addict.

Here's what that means in practice:

Don't use the language of addiction and recovery.
   • They never had the disease of addiction, and so they can't relapse into the disease, and they can't recover from it.

• They've been under the belief that they need heavy substance use to be happy, and like all people with all things, they may grow to believe they'll be happier living differently.

• They aren't in a battle against addiction, they are on a quest to figure out what life choices will make them happiest. If they're intermittently using heavily or not, it's either because they're fully happy with this choice, or they're still unsure of whether a life of less turbulent substance use can be happier for them.

• You can be supportive by discussing their past problems as a matter of choice, and their changes as a matter of choice and personal discovery/growth.

Stop asking for them to justify their use of substances.

• If you ask for a justification, they will give you one that they believe is palatable to you and socially acceptable for those in the role of the helpless addict. They'll tell you they were too angry, sad, depressed, or anxious and that this forced them to use substances.

• The more they use these excuses, the more real the excuses become to them, but the fact is that they used substances simply because they preferred to use them. They thought it would make them happy. The sooner they face this reality, the sooner they can take ownership of their choices and stop feeling helplessly pushed into substance use.

• If you don't ask for, or entertain those excuses, they will be left to simply assess how well their substance use choices are working out for them. If the subject of their substance use arises, you can ask them, much like our Presenters, how happy it is making them, and what might make them happier.

• This is incredibly supportive of their new role as a capable person freely choosing their own behavior.

Don't always assume the worst, and don't even out the costs.

• Many heroin users become moderate drinkers or marijuana users. At least 50% of heavy drinkers become moderate drinkers. People can and do moderate their use of substances.

• As they explore these adjustments to their substance use, one thing that figures into whether the change is "worth it" and makes them happier, is the social reaction to their changes. If the people in their life react to them having one fun night of a few drinks exactly the same as if they went on a weeklong binge of drinking, and then make the rest of the week miserable for them, this can alter their assessment of their substance use options.

• They might react to this a few ways, by thinking that a single night of drinking moderately isn't worth it because of the family's reaction and decide not to do it again; or they might think that if one night of moderate drinking is going to be treated like a week of nonstop drinking, then they might as well continue drinking for a week; or they might react by thinking that they need to get better at hiding their moderate use, at the cost of keeping distance from their loved ones. And there are plenty more reactions to be had. But the point is this: if you even out the costs of all substance use, you could help to make heavier substance use more attractive.

• Think of it this way, if all cuts of beef were the same price per pound—from ground chuck, to sirloin, all the way up to Kobe beef filet mignon, you'd buy nothing but that tender filet mignon whenever you want beef. In substance use terms, this means that if a single joint, beer, or snort of cocaine has the same costs as a fifth of whiskey, gram of cocaine, or a week of heavy drinking or IV heroin use, then what would you choose when you have a preference for being high? You'd probably say to hell with it, and go with the extreme levels of use.

Remember, you don't have to accept or be happy with any level of substance use from your loved ones. You are entitled to be happy in your life as well. But if you impose the same costs on your loved one for all levels of substance use—from the lowest levels to heavy usage, and those costs are important to them, it may make more sense to them to get the biggest bang for their buck.

After learning The Freedom Model, substance users aren't fragile, but they are still in a process of discovery about whether or not they can be happier making a change in their substance use habits. You can be supportive of this process by allowing them to make their discoveries without continuously policing them and demanding that they conform to your preferences.

With that being said, you are free to make the choices you need to make that you believe will make you happy. You can make these choices knowing full well that the only person you can control is yourself. No matter how hard you try, you can't save anyone from him or herself, and you are completely incapable of directing another person's choices, behaviors or preferences.

While you may certainly feel that you will be happier if your loved one chooses abstinence, this is not your choice to make, so it is crucial for your own happiness that you find a way past it and begin focusing on things in your life directly under your control.

CHAPTER 9:

BREAKING FREE: IT'S YOUR TURN

The Freedom Model for the Family has touched on some of the life-transforming information covered in *The Freedom Model for Addictions*, and it has also adapted those topics to help you, the family and friends of the substance user. For far too long you may have been operating under a cloud of myths, misinformation, outright lies and distortions perpetrated by well-meaning mental health and addiction treatment professionals, our culture and the substance user.

You have now learned that addiction, as defined by modern psychology and treatment professionals, does not exist. You have learned there is no disease that renders people powerless over substances and over their thoughts and behaviors. You have learned alcohol and drugs have no power to enslave people, not on their own and not even when ingested. And you have learned not only does the substance user have the power to change and always has, but so do you.

Whether the substance user is your child, spouse or significant other, sibling, parent, employee, or close friend, you now know the limits of your personal power with respect to their behavior. No matter how much you may want to control the substance user, your efforts are in vain. Nobody can control anyone but themselves and, ultimately, this means no one can save anyone from themselves.

People will always have what our society considers to be vices, whether it's driving too fast, eating sweets, facebooking incessantly, Internet shopping, substance use or any one of the thousands of behaviors our families and society deem irritating, morally wrong, bad or dangerous. Very few of us do not have at least one behavior that we or others would like us to change.

You know for yourself the minute you are told you must change a behavior, it becomes that much more difficult to change. If a doctor recommends cutting red meat and fats out of your diet, you may end up wanting it more. You may even find yourself craving it, not because of an addiction, but simply because you are devoting so much thought to what you were told you can't have but still want. The truth is, you can have red meat and you can eat greasy French fries, but your health will likely suffer. The choice is yours and yours alone. But you can also re-assess your preference for red meat and French fries and decide if you are willing to pay the price for the benefits you will get. You can assess if you may be happier with less or with none at all.

When moral judgment is stripped away from simple behaviors then a clear picture of choice, benefits and costs emerges. When your loved one gets drunk or high they are making that choice based on what they perceive will bring them happiness. When they choose to be abstinent or reduce their substance use, this choice is also made in the pursuit of personal happiness. The good news for you is you are also free to make a choice based on what you think will make you happy. You can do this free from concerns your loved one is sick or powerless because he or she is not, and you can do this free from guilt, shame or worry. It is time for you to build and live the life you have always wanted. By doing so, you will become an amazing power of example for everyone around you, including the substance user you are trying to help.

REFERENCES

Baldwin Research Institute. *Results of follow up surveys for Saint Jude Program Graduates.* http://www.soberforever.net/program_success1.cfm retrieved October 6, 2012.

Center for Behavioral Health Statistics and Quality. (2016). *Key substance use and mental health indicators in the United States: Results from the 2015 national survey on drug use and health* (HHS Publication No. SMA 16-4984, NSDUH Series H-51). Retrieved from https://www.samhsa.gove/data/sites/default/files/NSDUH-FFR1-2015Rev1/NSDUH-Nationalfindings-Revised-2015.pdf.

Getlen, L. (2013, April 21). *The Kennedy meth.* Retrieved from http://nypost.com/2013/04/21/the-kennedy-meth/.

Kirsch, I. (2010). *The emporer's new drugs: Exploding the antidepressant myth* (p. 19-20) [Kindle edition]. New York, NY: Perseus Books Group.

Lopez-Quintero, C., Hasin, D. S., de los Cobos, J. P., Pines, A., Wang, S., Grant, B. F. and Blanco, C. (2011), Probability and predictors of remission from life-time nicotine, alcohol, cannabis or cocaine dependence: results from the National Epidemiologic Survey on Alcohol and Related Conditions. Addiction, 106: 657–669. doi:10.1111/j.1360-0443.2010.03194.x

Miller, W.R., Westerberg, V. S., Harris, R. J. & Tonigan, J. S. (1996) *What predicts relapse? Prospective testing of antecedent models.* Addiction (Abingdon, England), 91 (Suppl), S155-172.

Scheeren, M., Slate, S. & Dunbar, M. (2017) *The freedom model for addictions: Escape the treatment and recovery trap.* Amsterdam, NY: BRI Publishing.

Sobell, L. C., Cunningham, J. A., & Sobell, M. B. (1996). *Recovery from alcohol problems with and without treatment: prevalence in two population surveys.* American Journal of Public Health, 86(7), 966-972.

Sullum, J. (2014, February 20). *Hyperbole hurts: the surprising truth about methamphetamine.* Retrieved from https://www.forebes.com/sites/jacobsullum/2014/02/20/hyperbole-hurts-the-surprising-truth-about-methamphetamine/#578dabb229f1.

Weil, A. (1998). *The natural mind: A new way of looking at drugs and the higher consciousness* (rev ed.). Boston, MA: Mariner Books.

Wilcox, S. (2015, June 27). *Alcohol, drugs, and crime.* Retrieved from https://www.ncadd.org/about-addiction/alcohol-drugs-crime.

Zinberg, N. (1984). *Drug, set and setting: The basis for controlled intoxicant use.* New Haven, CT: Yale University. Retrived from https://doi.org/10.1080/02791072.1984.10524320

Made in the USA
Monee, IL
05 November 2023

45851084R00072

Made in the USA
Monee, IL
05 November 2023

45851084R00072